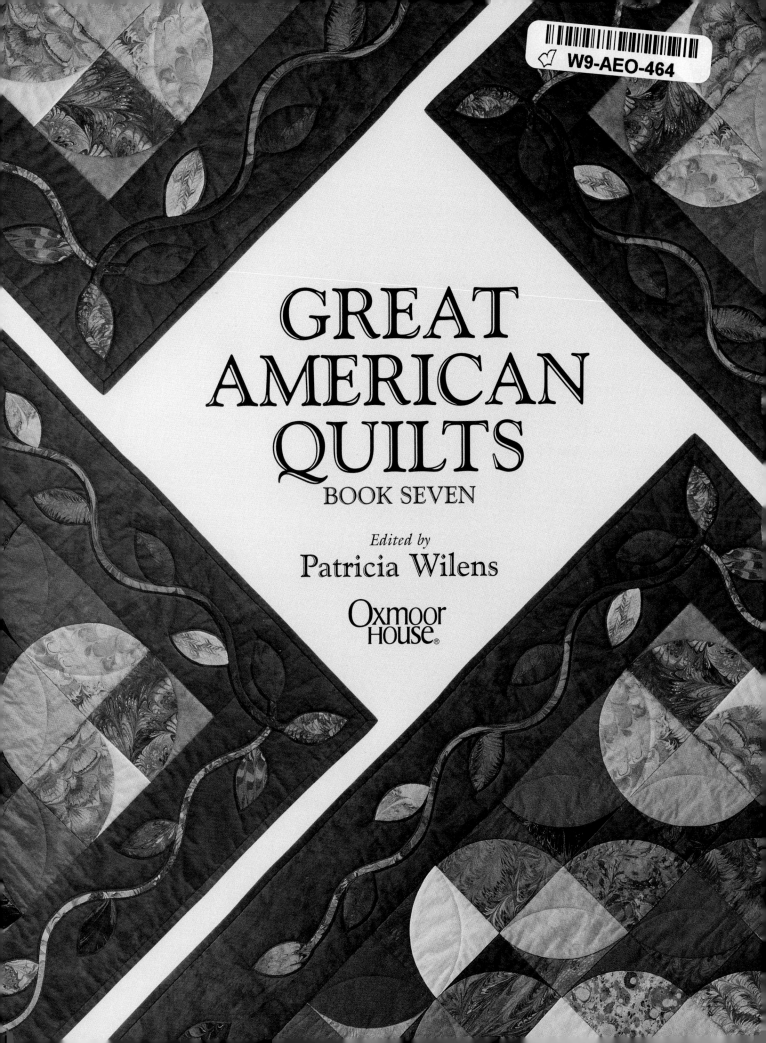

GREAT AMERICAN QUILTS

BOOK SEVEN

Edited by

Patricia Wilens

Oxmoor
HOUSE®

Great American Quilts Book Seven

©1999 by Oxmoor House, Inc.
Book Division of Southern Progress Corporation
P.O. Box 2463, Birmingham, Alabama 35201

Published by Oxmoor House, Inc., and Leisure Arts, Inc.

Library of Congress Catalog Card Number: 86-62283
ISBN: 0-8487-1893-3
ISSN: 1076-7673
Printed in the United States of America
First Printing 1999

Editor-in-Chief: Nancy Fitzpatrick Wyatt
Senior Crafts Editor: Susan Ramey Cleveland
Senior Editor, Copy and Homes: Olivia Kindig Wells
Art Director: James Boone

Great American Quilts Book Seven
Editor: Patricia Wilens
Contributing Copy Editor: Susan S. Cheatham
Contributing Designer: Barbara Ball
Illustrator: Kelly Davis
Senior Photographer: John O'Hagan
Photo Stylist: Linda Baltzell Wright
Publishing Systems Administrator: Rick Tucker
Director, Production and Distribution: Phillip Lee
Associate Production Manager: Theresa L. Beste
Production Assistant: Faye Porter Bonner

We're Here for You!
We at Oxmoor House are dedicated to serving you with reliable information that expands your imagination and enriches your life. We welcome your comments and suggestions. Please write us at:

Oxmoor House, Inc.
Editor, *Great American Quilts 2000*
2100 Lakeshore Drive
Birmingham, AL 35209
To order additional publications, call 1-205-877-6560.

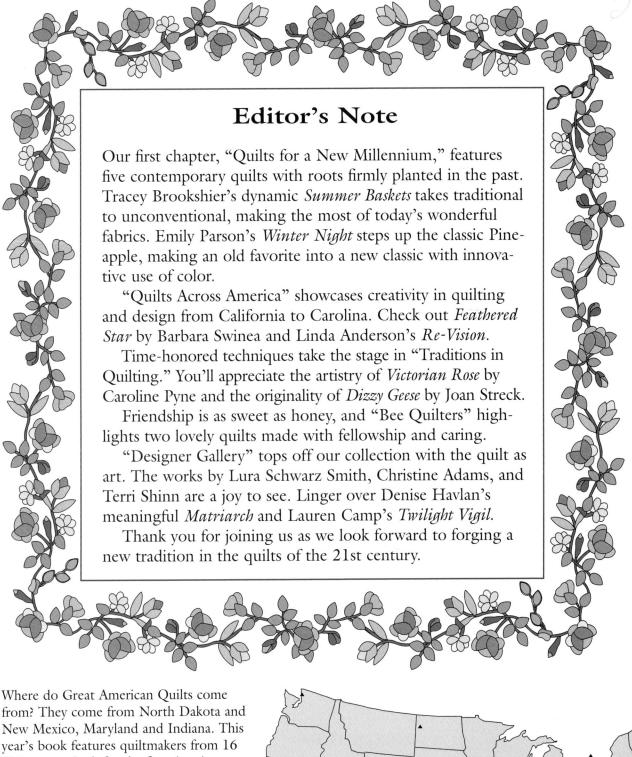

Editor's Note

Our first chapter, "Quilts for a New Millennium," features five contemporary quilts with roots firmly planted in the past. Tracey Brookshier's dynamic *Summer Baskets* takes traditional to unconventional, making the most of today's wonderful fabrics. Emily Parson's *Winter Night* steps up the classic Pineapple, making an old favorite into a new classic with innovative use of color.

"Quilts Across America" showcases creativity in quilting and design from California to Carolina. Check out *Feathered Star* by Barbara Swinea and Linda Anderson's *Re-Vision*.

Time-honored techniques take the stage in "Traditions in Quilting." You'll appreciate the artistry of *Victorian Rose* by Caroline Pyne and the originality of *Dizzy Geese* by Joan Streck.

Friendship is as sweet as honey, and "Bee Quilters" highlights two lovely quilts made with fellowship and caring.

"Designer Gallery" tops off our collection with the quilt as art. The works by Lura Schwarz Smith, Christine Adams, and Terri Shinn are a joy to see. Linger over Denise Havlan's meaningful *Matriarch* and Lauren Camp's *Twilight Vigil*.

Thank you for joining us as we look forward to forging a new tradition in the quilts of the 21st century.

Where do Great American Quilts come from? They come from North Dakota and New Mexico, Maryland and Indiana. This year's book features quiltmakers from 16 U.S. states. And, for the first time in our 14-year history, we welcome Canada to the family of continental American quilters.

If your state isn't represented this year, pledge to make a mark on next year's map. To submit a quilt, please send a snapshot with your name, address, and phone number to *Great American Quilts* Editor, Oxmoor House, 2100 Lakeshore Drive, Birmingham, AL 35209. Deadline for the 2001 edition is January 7, 2000.

Quilts for a New Millenium

Quilts Across America

Traditions in Quilting

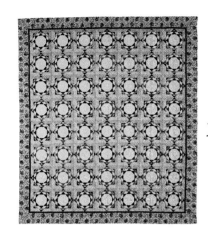

Bee Quilters

Designer Gallery

Quilt Smart

Quilts for a New Millenium

Tracey M. Brookshier
Capitola, California

*T*racey Brookshier likes bold, bright, way-out, in-your-face *color.* "My favorite part of quilting is choosing fabrics to go in a quilt," Tracey says, "and my favorite quilts have lots of different fabrics."

Interpreting traditional blocks in bright, contemporary fabrics is Tracey's forté. She likes big quilts that make a strong visual impact.

"My favorite part of quilting is choosing fabrics."

Tracey sews almost every day, and she enjoys quilt shows. "I eavesdrop on people's comments," Tracey admits. "It's fun to hear one person say a quilt doesn't do a thing for her, and then the next person says, 'I just *love* this.' " Variation of expression, from traditional to way-out art, is what Tracey finds so exciting in quiltmaking.

Tracey is a member of the Pajaro Valley Quilt Association of Santa Cruz County. She also quilts with the Sew Little Timers and the Bent Needles.

Summer Baskets
1996

Summer Baskets is the first in a series of quilts inspired by one sumptuous fabric.

"I loved the large floral," Tracey says of P&B's Alhambra print. Four luscious colorways inspired her to make a basket quilt for each season. The print sets the tone for each quilt, letting Tracey stir up a rainbow of bright fabrics to complement each print.

The basket is a combination of two traditional blocks. "The same fabric in the center of each basket brings order" to a busy scrap quilt, Tracey says. The border showcases the unifying fabric in all its glory.

Tracey's quilts were shown at the Marin Quilt & Needle Arts Show, the Pajaro Valley Quilt Fair, and the Pacific International Quilt Festival.

Summer Baskets

Finished Size
Quilt: 85¾" x 100"
Blocks: 50 (10" x 10")

Materials
2¾ yards print border fabric
1½ yards coordinating fabric
 (lime) for setting triangles
⅜ yard inner border fabric
50 (7" x 13") basket fabrics*
49 (6" x 21") tone-on-tone
 prints for block backgrounds*
1 yard binding fabric
2⅝ yards 108"-wide backing
*Note: In Tracey's quilt, no fabric is repeated. You can substitute 17 fat quarters for baskets and another 17 fat quarters for block backgrounds.

Pieces to Cut
Cutting and piecing instructions are for rotary cutting. For traditional piecing, use patterns on pages 12 and 13. Cut all strips cross-grain except as noted.

From border fabric
• 4 (6¾" x 90") lengthwise strips for outer border.
• 25 (6⅞") squares. Cut each square in half diagonally to get 50 A triangles.

From setting fabric
• 5 (15½") squares. Cut each square in quarters diagonally to get 18 setting triangles (and 2 extra).
• 2 (8") squares. Cut each square in half diagonally to get 4 corner triangles.

Machine-quilted by Laura Lee Fritz of Napa, California.

From each basket fabric
• 1 (6⅞") square. Cut square in half to get 1 A triangle. Discard extra triangle or use for another block.

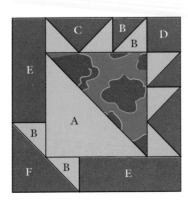

Basket Block—Make 50.

• 2 (2⅞") squares. Cut 1 square in half to get 2 B triangles. Save second square for triangle-squares.
• 4 (2½") squares for B piecing.

From binding fabric
• 1 (32") square for bias binding. Add remainder to block background fabrics.

From each background fabric
• 1 (5") square. Cut square in half diagonally to get 1 F triangle. Discard extra triangle or use for another block.
• 1 (2⅞") square for B triangle-squares.
• 2 (2½" x 6½") E pieces.
• 2 (2½" x 4½") C pieces.
• 1 (2½") D square.

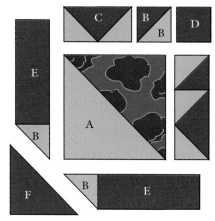

Block Assembly Diagram

Quilt Top Assembly

1. For each block, select a set of A and B basket pieces, a set of B, C, D, E, F background pieces, and 1 border print A triangle *(Block Assembly Diagram)*. Join A triangles; press seam allowances toward basket fabric.

2. Lightly mark a diagonal line on wrong side of 1 (2⅞") B square of basket fabric. Match this with same-size square of background fabric, right sides facing. Stitch ¼" seam on *both* sides of line *(Diagram A)*. Press. Cut apart on drawn line to get 2 B triangle-squares.

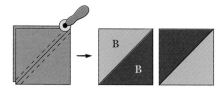

Diagram A

3. See Quilt Smart (page 91) for instructions for on Diagonal-Corners Quick-Piecing technique. Use this method to sew 2½" squares to corners of each C rectangle *(Diagram B)*.

4. Sew B triangles to ends of each E piece, making sure triangles point in opposite directions as shown.

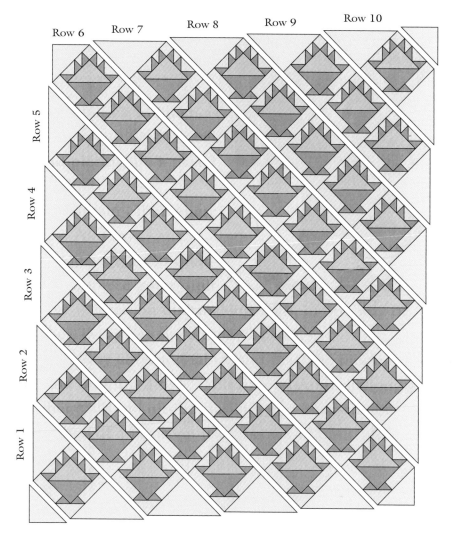

Quilt Top Assembly Diagram

5. Lay out units *(Block Assembly Diagram)*. Join B triangle-square to end of B/C unit at side of block. Sew combined unit to right edge of A square.

6. Join D, B triangle-square, and B/C unit. Sew combined unit to top edge of block.

7. Sew B/E strips to left and bottom edges as shown. Then sew F triangle to bottom left corner to complete block. Make 50 blocks.

8. Lay out blocks in 10 diagonal rows *(Quilt Top Assembly Diagram)*. End rows with setting triangles as shown. Move blocks around to achieve a nice balance of color and fabrics. When satisfied with block placement, join blocks and triangles in each row.

9. Join rows to complete quilt center. Sew corner triangles in place as shown.

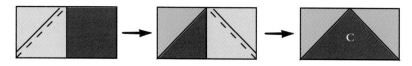

Diagram B

11

Borders

1. Cut 8 (1½"-wide) strips of inner border fabric. Sew 2 strips end-to-end for each border.
2. Measure length of quilt through center of quilt top. Trim 2 border strips to match length. Sew these to quilt sides, easing to fit as needed. Press seam allowances toward borders. Repeat for top and bottom borders.
3. Add outer border strips in same manner.

Quilting and Finishing

Quilt shown is outline-quilted by machine and additional free-motion quilting (with red thread!) put hearts and curlicues around baskets.

Bind with straight-grain or bias binding made from remaining binding fabric.

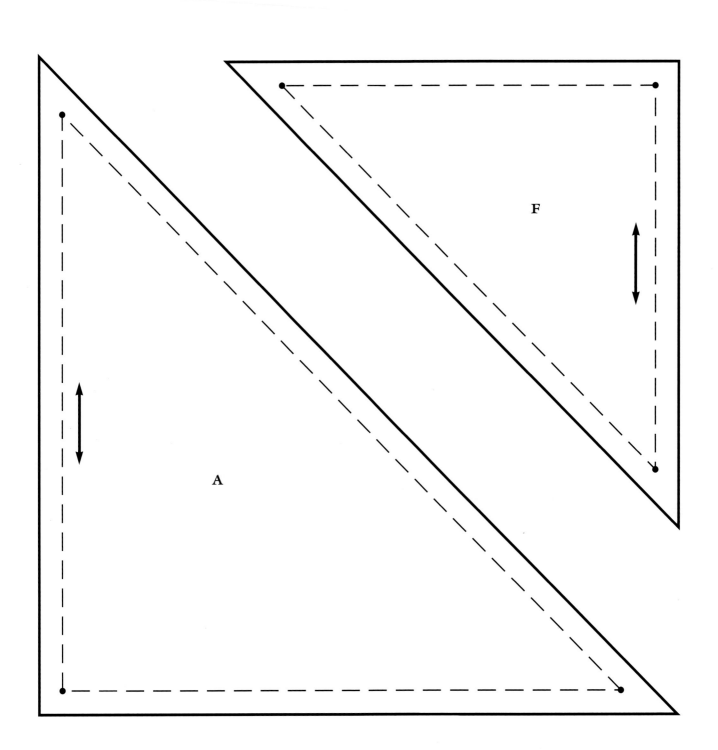

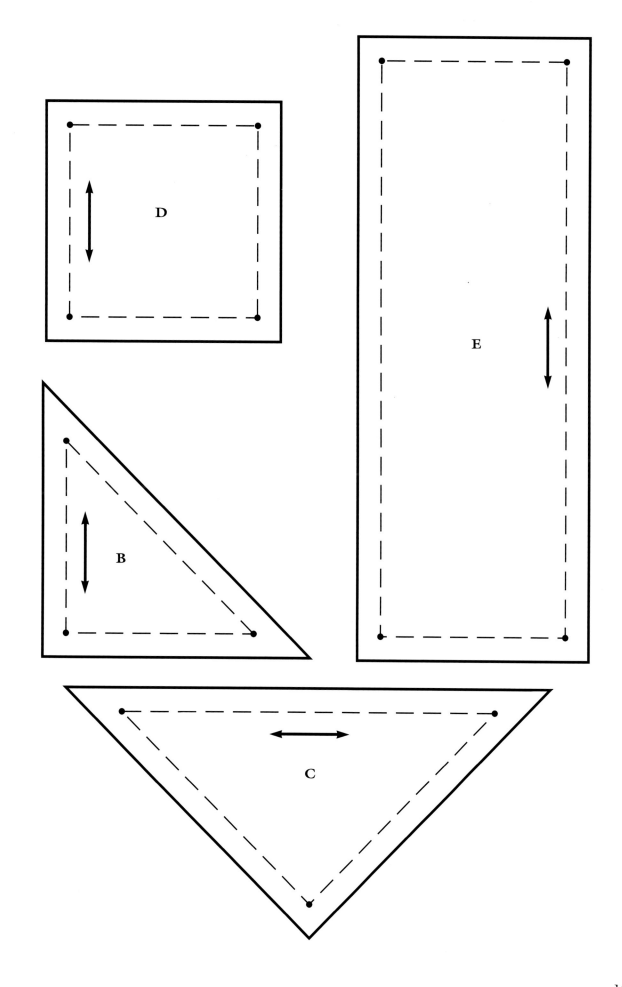

Christine L. Adams
Rockville, Maryland

*F*abric and texture have always been part of Christine Adams's life. Tied scraps were a favorite childhood toy. "As I grew up, my methods for holding 'artwork' together became more sophisticated," Christine says, "so along the way, I learned to sew and now I quilt."

"There is always . . . a new wrinkle to smooth— or not, as I choose."

Playing with fabric is now Christine's main pursuit. After teaching in the Montgomery County public schools, she decided to fulfill her dreams in fiber art.

"I can continue this love affair with fiber begun when I was very young," says Christine. "There is always a new approach to try and a new wrinkle to smooth—or not, as I choose."

Christine's current passion is color and free-motion quilting. She says, "For me, the term 'free-motion quilting' gives legitimacy to free-form scribbling, and I do it all over my quilts!"

At Rockville Arts Place, Christine shares studio space with 13 artists who exchange ideas and techniques in other media. Christine is a member of the American Quilters' Society, Studio Art Quilt Association, and the Fiber Art Study Group.

For a look at more of Christine's work, see *Our Town,* on page 133.

Celebration
1998

This is one of a series of quilts inspired by the seasons. *Celebration* embraces the exuberance of a blossoming spring and the coming of summer. Other quilts in the series (shown on page 17) herald Indian summer and winter.

These quilts are among many Christine has made using bold color, geometric shapes, and contemporary techniques of fusible appliqué and free-motion quilting.

While the upbeat, colorful look of this quilt is just as fun if it's made traditionally, the fusible technique is fast and fun. And it's sturdy enough to withstand the wear and tear of daily use. Try this type of appliqué for a quilt that will be used in a college dorm, for example—you can make something "way cool" that doesn't have to last more than four years.

Celebration

Finished Size

Quilt: 38" x 38"
Blocks: 100 (3¾" x 3¾")

Materials

164 (4¼") scrap squares or
    17 (9" x 22") fat eighths in
    assorted "springtime" colors
⅜ yard binding fabric
1¼ yards backing fabric
1 yard paper-backed fusible
    web (optional)

Pieces to Cut

Instructions are for rotary cutting and fusible appliqué.
Before cutting, read instructions below and on page 18 to decide if you prefer fusible or traditional appliqué. Appliqué patterns are on page 17.

From scrap fabrics

• 100 (4¼") squares for
  background.

• 64 (4¼") squares for appliqué.

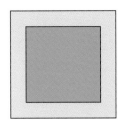

Square Block—Make 32.

Circle Block—Make 32.

Other quilts in Christine's seasonal series: Tough Sledding *(winter) at left, and* Firelight *(fall) at right. Use* Celebration *patterns for* Firelight; *patterns for* Tough Sledding *not available.*

Quilt Top Assembly

1. Referring to photo, arrange 10 horizontal rows of fabric squares, with 10 squares in each row. Experiment with placement and position of fabrics until you have a layout that is balanced and pleasing. Do not sew rows together until appliqué is complete.

2. See Quilt Smart instructions on page 18 for tips on fusible appliqué. Trace 32 circles and 32 squares onto paper side of fusible web. Cut out web pieces, leaving a small amount of paper around each outline.

3. Fuse a web piece to wrong side of each remaining fabric square. Cut out appliqués on drawn line.

4. Referring to photo, arrange appliqués on center 8 rows of foundation squares, alternating groups of 4 circles with groups of 4 squares. When satisfied with color and fabric placement, fuse appliqués onto foundation squares 1 at a time, returning each finished block to its correct place in the layout.

5. Join blocks in rows; then join rows to complete quilt top.

Quilting and Finishing

For free-motion machine quilting, Christine used blue thread to "scribble" squiggly stitching lines over seams and over and around appliqués. The more wobbly the stitching, the more creative you are. Or quilt traditionally, if desired.

Make straight-grain binding from coordinating fabric.

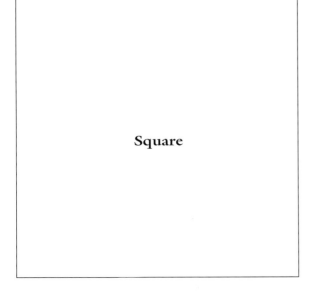

Square

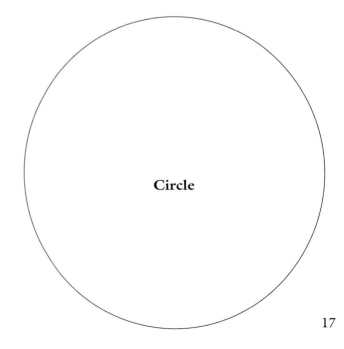

Circle

❖QUILT SMART❖

Fusible Appliqué

Paper-backed fusible web is a heat-activated adhesive with a temporary paper lining. Heated with a hot iron, fusible web secures appliqués to a background fabric.

Use lightweight web to appliqué wall hangings. For a washable quilt, heavy-duty web might be better. When you use fusible web, read the label for tips on use and washing. Before fusing, always prewash fabrics to remove sizing, which prevents fusible web from bonding with fabric.

Available brands of paper-backed web include Pellon® WonderUnder, Aleene's Fusible Web™, and HeatnBond®.

Fusing

1. With a pencil, trace motif onto paper (smooth) side of web *(Photo A)*. Use paper scissors to cut around motif, leaving a small amount of paper around the tracing.

2. Place adhesive (rough) side of web on *wrong* side of appliqué fabric. Following package instructions, use a dry iron to fuse web to fabric *(Photo B)*. Do not overheat. Some manufacturers recommend a pressing cloth between iron and appliqué to avoid getting stray fibers of sticky stuff on the iron.

3. Let fabric cool. Cut out motif on drawn line. If desired, use pinking shears for a jagged edge.

4. Peel paper backing from back of web *(Photo C)*.

5. Position appliqué on background. Be sure of placement before you fuse, following manufacturer's directions *(Photo D)*.

6. Fusible web holds appliqués in place through many washings, but it's best to finish edges to prevent fraying. You can topstitch or satin-stitch edges by machine, or add a buttonhole stitch by hand or by machine.

A

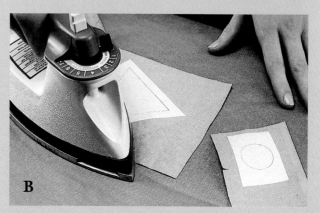

B

C

D

Sharon Gilmore-Thompson
Lamoille, Nevada

*I*t's interesting how life sometimes goes in circles. Sharon Gilmore-Thompson took her first quilting class at Great Basin College in 1983. Now she's the teacher.

"A broad palette of color and shape drives the creative appetite."

Sharon urges new students to have fun with color. "Bright fabrics seem to be forbidden fruit for new quilters," Sharon says. "I like to use bright, contemporary fabrics," she says, and she encourages students to use them, too. "I want my students to realize the possibilities beyond the pastels of our grandmothers' quilts."

For Sharon, quilting is now a consuming passion. "A broad palette of color and shape drives the creative appetite," Sharon believes. "It's what makes quilting so rewarding."

Sharon spends 40–50 hours a week on her own quilting. She recently started a home business doing machine quilting for others and finds it very rewarding. "Between teaching and quilting for others, I have the best of both worlds," she says.

Sharon is a member of the Winnemucca Crazy Quilters and two smaller bees.

When Life Gives You Oranges, Make a Quilt
1998

When Sharon Gilmore-Thompson sets out to teach a new pattern to her quilting students, use of color is a main focus.

When Life Gives You Oranges . . . is one of the quilts Sharon teaches beginner students. Inspired by a photo in a decorating magazine, she drafted the pattern, using a Monkey Wrench block. She purposely pieced it in colors that many people avoid.

Oranges, yellows, reds, and purples seem to be particularly scary. Students "might pull a bolt off the shelf to look at, but they feel uncomfortable with it," Sharon observes. Showing this example of how dynamic orange is when used skillfully takes the edge off a beginner's worries.

Sharon's quilt was shown at the 1998 Pacific International Quilt Festival.

When Life Gives You Oranges, Make a Quilt

Finished Size
Quilt: 76" x 89"
Blocks: 30 (10" x 10")

Materials
2¼ yards border fabric*
2 yards orange setting fabric
1⅜ yards sashing fabric
½ yard inner border fabric
20 (8" x 10") blue fabrics for stars
60 (8" x 10") scrap fabrics for blocks (assorted lights, mediums, and darks)
30 (2") scrap squares for blocks
1 yard binding fabric
5⅜ yards backing fabric
*Includes enough fabric for binding, if desired.

Pieces to Cut
Instructions are for rotary cutting.
From outer border fabric
•4 (6" x 81") lengthwise strips. Use remaining fabric for binding and/or patchwork, if desired.
From orange setting fabric
•60 (6¼") squares. Cut each square in quarters diagonally to get 120 C setting triangles.
From sashing fabric
•12 (3½"-wide) cross-grain strips. From these, cut 48 (3½" x 10½") sashing pieces. Do not trim ends yet.
From each blue fabric for stars
•1 (3½") square.
•4 (2¼" x 3⅞") pieces. Cut each piece in half diagonally *(Diagram A)* or make a template of Pattern X to cut 4 X and 4 X reversed.

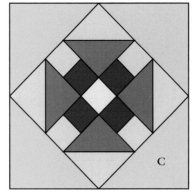

Monkey Wrench Block—Make 30.

From each scrap fabric
•60 (2" x 8") strips.
•60 (6" x 10") pieces.

Quilt Top Assembly
1. For 1 block, select 2 (2" x 8") strips, 2 (6" x 10") pieces, and a 2" square. One 2" x 8" and 1 (6" x 10") should be of same fabric for block background.
2. On wrong side of 1 (6" x 10") piece, draw 2 (3⅞") squares, leaving a 1" margin around markings *(Diagram B)*.

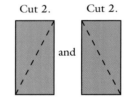

Diagram A

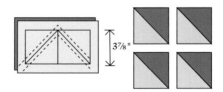

Diagram B

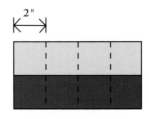

Diagram C

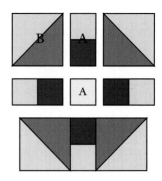

Block Assembly Diagram

Draw diagonal lines through squares as shown. Match marked fabric with second 6" x 10" piece, right sides facing. Stitch ¼" seam on *both* sides of diagonal lines as shown. Press. Cut apart on drawn lines to get 4 B triangle-squares.
3. Join 2" x 8" strips. From this, cut 4 (2"-wide) A segments *(Diagram C)*.
4. Lay out units in 3 horizontal rows *(Block Assembly Diagram)*, including 2" A center square. Join units in each row. Then join rows.
5. Sew orange C triangles to 2 opposite sides of block. Press. Then sew triangles to remaining sides. Triangles are slightly oversized, so second pair of triangles should slightly overlap first triangles at block corners.
6. Make 30 blocks. Trim each block to 10½" square, leaving a generous ¼" seam allowance on each side.
7. Lay out blocks in 6 horizontal rows, with 5 blocks in each row *(Row Assembly Diagram)*. Lay untrimmed sashings between blocks and between rows as shown. Move blocks around to achieve a nice balance of color and fabrics. When satisfied with

block placement, lay star pieces on top of sashing to determine star fabric placement.

8. For first row, use template of Sashing Pattern to trim 1 end only of each sashing strip. Sew X star points to end of each strip. Press seam allowances toward star points. Join blocks and sashing units in Row 1. Press seam allowances toward sashing. Assemble last row (Row 6) in same manner.

9. For Sashing Row, trim 1 end of first and last sashing strips and both ends of 3 center strips. Sew star points in place; press. Join sashing units and squares in a row as shown. Press seam allowances toward squares. Make 4 more sashing rows in same manner.

10. Trim both ends of 4 sashing strips in Block Row 2. Sew star points in place on sashing strips and press. Join blocks and sashing units in Row 2. Join rows 3, 4, and 5 in same manner.

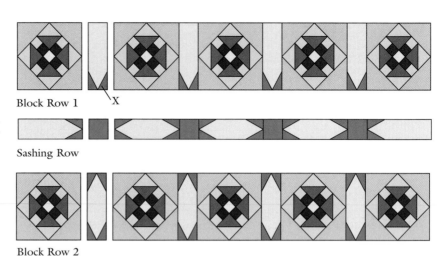

Block Row 1 X

Sashing Row

Block Row 2

Row Assembly Diagram

11. Referring to photo, join all rows to complete quilt center.

Borders

1. Cut 8 (2"-wide) strips of inner border fabric. Sew 2 strips end-to-end for each border.
2. Measure length of quilt through center of quilt top. Trim 2 border strips to match length. Sew these to quilt sides, easing to fit as needed. Press seam allowances toward borders. Repeat for top and bottom borders.
3. Add outer border strips in same manner.

Quilting and Finishing

Quilt shown is machine-quilted in a variety of overlapping circles. Quilt as desired.

Bind with straight-grain or bias binding.

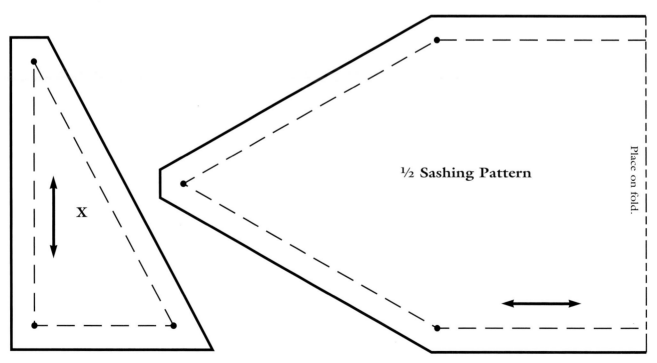

X

½ **Sashing Pattern**

Place on fold.

Peggy True
Clayton, California

Color. Variety. Fabric. Sharing. These are words of joy for Peggy True, because they are the essential ingredients of quiltmaking.

"Creative expression in fabric . . . is where I find my bliss."

Peggy says, "Creative expression in fabric, whether in quilts or garments, is where I find my bliss." Starting in the 1970s, Peggy learned the basics of hand piecing, appliqué, and hand quilting. That traditional foundation gradually expanded to include new, faster methods of translating her ideas into fabric. Now her sewing machine gets a daily workout.

Peggy enjoyed being a "mom-at-home" for many years, but now an empty nest gives her more time to devote to quilting and teaching.

"Teaching is its own reward," Peggy says. "I love the camaraderie we share as creative women, the exchange of ideas, and the mutual support."

Peggy is the author of a book on patchwork jackets. She is a member of the Guild of Quilters of Contra Costa County and several national quilters' organizations.

Anthem Autumnal
1997

Collecting fabric is hardly a habit unique to Peggy True. Nor is it unusual to have no specific quilt in mind as the collection takes shape. It's *having* the fabric that counts. And sometimes the fabric determines its own fate.

Peggy purchased some hand-marbled cottons by artist Marjorie Lee Bevins and some suede-look cotton solids in the autumnal palette, not knowing what she would make of them. She eventually settled on the idea of a quilt that would suggest autumn foliage in all its glory.

"I love how the two kinds of fabrics complement each other," Peggy says.

She designed a quarter-circle two-patch similar to a traditional Drunkard's Path. Then Peggy added a simple undulating vine-and-leaf border that repeats the curves of the piecing. "I believe the repetition brings unity to the quilt's design," she says.

Anthem Autumnal won the "Golden Bear" award for best quilt at the 1997 California State Fair. It also garnered awards at the 1998 Mid-Atlantic Quilt Festival and the 1998 Marin County Quilt and Needle Arts Show. The quilt was shown at the 1997 Pacific International Quilt Festival and the 1998 International Quilt Festival in Houston.

Anthem Autumnal

Finished Size
Quilt: 70" x 70"
Blocks: 169 (4½" x 4½")

Materials
2 yards green solid border fabric
3 (⅓-yard) pieces marbled
    fabrics for vine and leaves
22 (¼-yard) pieces marbeled
    fabrics for blocks
21 (¼-yard) pieces solid fabrics
 4¼ yards backing fabric
¼"-wide bias pressing bar

Pieces to Cut
From border fabric
• 4 (6" x 66") lengthwise strips
  for border.
• 2 (22") squares for binding.
Add remaining border fabric to
solid fabrics for patchwork.
From marbeled fabrics for blocks
• 85 of Pattern X.
• 84 of Pattern Y.
From solid fabrics
• 84 of Pattern X.
• 85 of Pattern Y.

Quilt Top Assembly
1. See Quilt Smart instructions
on page 29 for tips on piecing a
curved seam. Sew a marbeled X
piece to each solid Y to make 85
of Block 1 *(Block 1 Diagram)*.
Make 84 of Block 2 with solid
Xs and marbled Ys *(Block 2 Diagram)*. Press seam allowances
toward Y.

2. Referring to photo, arrange
blocks in 13 horizontal rows,
with 13 blocks in each row.
Experiment with placement and
position of blocks until you
have a layout that is balanced
and pleasing.
3. Join blocks in rows; then join
rows to complete quilt center.

Borders
1. Measure middle of quilt from
top to bottom and from side to
side. It's likely that your quilt is
not exactly square. Add 5¾" to
shorter measurement; trim border strips to this length.
2. Borders are attached in log-
cabin style. Match 1 border strip

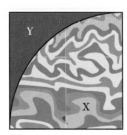

Block 1—Make 85.

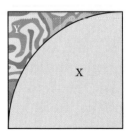

Block 2—Make 84.

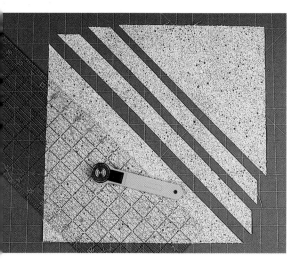

Photo A

to left side of quilt top, right sides facing. (Border will be longer than quilt at bottom.) Sew border strip to quilt side, stopping about 3" from bottom corner of quilt. Press seam allowance toward border.

3. Match 1 border strip to top of quilt, right sides facing. (Border should match quilt top.) Sew border strip to top edge, easing to fit as necessary. Press seam allowance toward border. Repeat for right side border; then sew bottom border.

4. Complete seam at left side, stitching over bottom border to finish border corners.

5. Cut 2 (12") squares from *each* ⅓-yard marbled piece. Cut squares in half diagonally to get 12 triangles. Cut 2 (⅝"-wide) bias strips from cut edge of each triangle to get a total of 24 strips *(Photo A)*. Cut 56 leaves (Pattern Z) from remaining fabric, adding seam allowances as you cut.

6. For each vine, select 1 bias strip of each fabric. Sew 3 bias strips end-to-end to get a continuous bias strip approximately 32½" long for each vine. Trim seam allowances to ⅛".

7. Fold each bias strip in thirds over pressing bar, right sides out. Press to make 8 (¼"-wide) vines.

8. Pin a leaf in 1 corner, referring to photo and *Border Diagram*. Pin second leaf just below it, straddling border seam. Pin a vine end under each leaf and wiggle each vine toward center of quilt, pinning curves in place. Pin leaves at end of each vine and in each curve, alternating leaves above and below vine as shown. Turn quilt to repeat vine placement at each corner. You should have about 2½" between leaves at center of each border.

9. Adjust vines and leaves until satisfied with placement. Sew 8 vines in place. Then appliqué all leaves.

Quilting and Finishing

Outline-quilt seams and around vines and leaves. Quilt curve through each X piece as shown on pattern.

Make straight-grain binding made from remaining fabric.

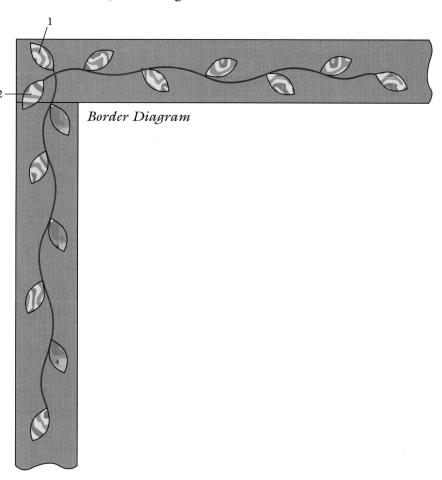

Border Diagram

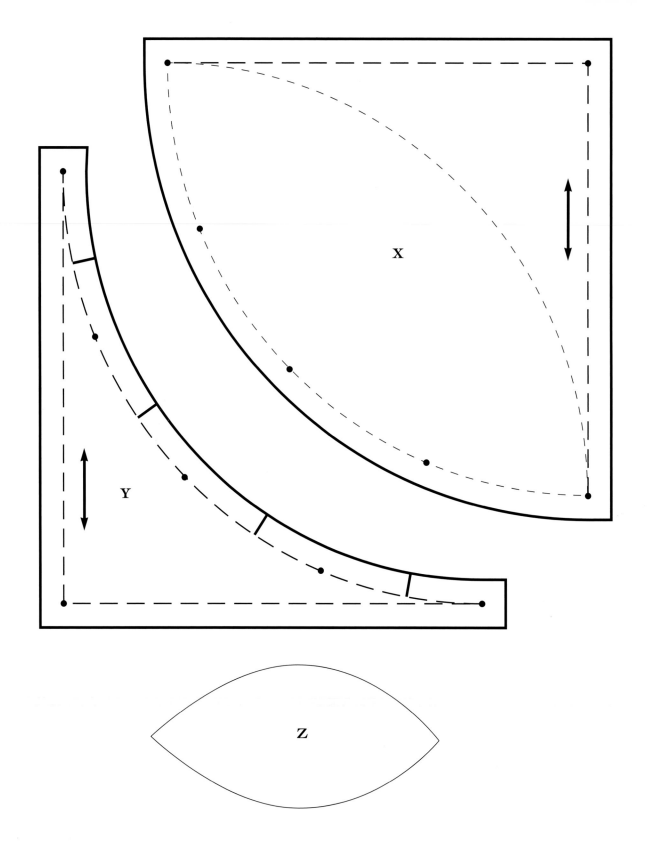

X

Y

Z

❖QUILT SMART❖

Piecing a Curved Seam

Curved piecing requires a little extra care to ensure a smooth, accurate seam. Try making a few practice units, using the methods described below, to see which technique you like best.

Hand or Machine Piecing

1. On each Y piece, make small clips between dots as shown on pattern. Be careful not to cut into seam line. Clips allow seam allowance to spread so curved edges will match for piecing.

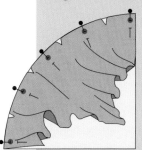

2. Match an X and a Y, right sides facing. Pin curved edges together, matching dots *(Diagram 1)*. Let Y gather as necessary, but

Diagram 1

make it as smooth as possible at curved edge.

3. With Y on top, stitch curved seam. Start at one end and carefully sew around curve, smoothing creases away from seam as you go. Remove each pin before you sew over it.

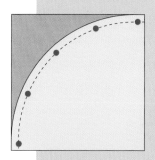

4. Press seam allowances toward Y *(Diagram 2)*. If necessary, a hot iron can work out tiny puckers in the seam.

Diagram 2

Appliqué

1. Make a pressing template for piece X. Use Templar (a heat-resistant, translucent sheet available at quilt shops or from mail-order sources) or a lightweight aluminum such as the bottom of a disposable pie pan. Cut pressing template with seam allowances on straight edges but not on curves *(Diagram 3)*.

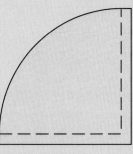

Diagram 3

2. Place fabric X piece facedown on ironing board. Spray curved edge with water or spray starch. Place template on fabric, aligning straight edges *(Diagram 4)*. Use tip of iron to press curved seam allowance over template edge. (If using aluminum, keep fingers away from template—metal will be hot at pressed edge.) Remove template when seam allowance is dry.

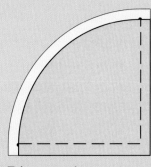

Diagram 4

3. Pin X to Y, aligning straight edges *(Diagram 5)*.

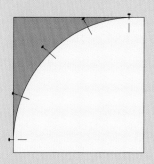

Diagram 5

4. Using thread that matches X, appliqué curved edge with a hand blindstitch *(Diagram 6)* or machine topstitch *(Diagram 7)*.

Diagram 6

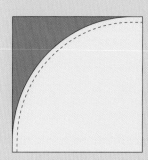

Diagram 7

29

Emily Parson
St. Charles, Illinois

*H*ow many of us have faith in things like fortune cookies? Emily Parson has good reason to believe—in college, she opened one that predicted, "Colors and textures will become important to you." That prophecy came true.

Emily always enjoyed sewing and crafts, and she'd seen her grandmother's traditional quilts. She was inspired to become a quiltmaker in 1991 when she saw an exhibit of art quilts at New York's Museum of American Folk Art. The quilt she finished the following year was the first of many.

"I've played with fabric all my life."

"I've played with fabric all my life," Emily says. She is inspired by things near and dear—family, pets, and her collection of "oddball household objects." She says she also finds inspiration in nature and "the places I've lived, especially city life."

You can see more of Emily's work on page 135.

Winter Night
1996

Everything old *can* be made new again. Just look at what Emily Parson does with a traditional Pineapple block, one of her favorites. She says, "I love to change traditional color placement to form new and unexpected shapes."

Daring use of color is a hallmark of an Emily Parson quilt, and her Pineapples are no exception. "I created this design in the fall, anticipating a cold Chicago winter," Emily says. "I finished it just before the first snowflakes fell."

Foundation-pieced and machine-quilted, *Winter Night* evokes the drama of a dark and stormy night illuminated by silent snowfall.

Winter Night won Best Use of Color at the 1997 Mid-Atlantic Quilt Festival and was shown at the American Quilters' Society show; Quilter's Heritage Celebration in Lancaster, Pennsylvania; and at the National Quilt Association show in Syracuse, New York.

30

Winter Night

Finished Size
Quilt: 84" x 84"
Blocks: 25 (14" x 14")
Half-Blocks: 20 (7" x 14")

Materials
Scraps or 36 (¼-yard) pieces
   black, dark gray, dark blue,
   and dark purple prints
Scraps or 9 (⅛-yard) pieces of
   white tone-on-tone fabrics
Scraps or 9 (⅛-yard) pieces of
   light purple fabrics
Scraps or 4 (⅛-yard) pieces of
   light gray fabrics
2½ yards 90"-wide backing fabric
Pad of 18" x 24" tracing paper

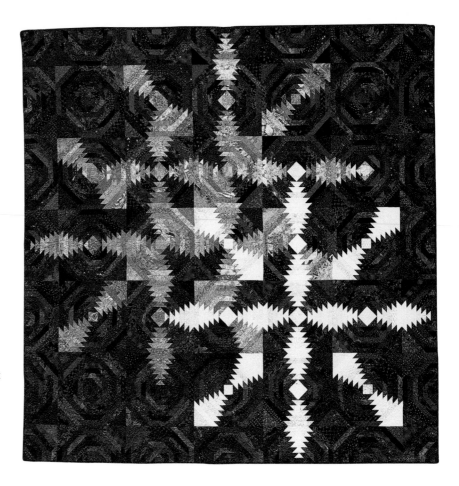

Pieces to Cut
Cut all strips cross-grain.
From assorted dark fabrics
- 60 (4") squares. Cut each
  square in half diagonally to get
  120 M triangles.
- 25 (3¼") squares. Cut each
  square in quarters diagonally
  to get 100 A triangles.
- 4 (2½") squares for block centers (blocks 2B, 2F, 6B, 6C).
- 20 (1½" x 2½") pieces for
  half-block centers.
- 4 (1½") squares for corner-
  block centers.
- 180 (1½"-wide) strips.

From assorted white fabrics
- 4 (4") squares. Cut each
  square in half diagonally to get
  8 M triangles.
- 7 (3¼") squares. Cut each
  square in quarters diagonally to
  get 26 A triangles (and 2 extra).
- 10 (2½") squares for block
  centers.
- 21 (1½"-wide) strips.

From assorted light purple fabrics
- 4 (4") squares. Cut each
  square in half diagonally to get
  8 M triangles.
- 5 (3¼") squares. Cut each
  square in quarters diagonally to
  get 19 A triangles (and 1 extra).
- 7 (2½") squares for block
  centers.
- 21 (1½"-wide) strips.

From assorted gray fabrics
- 4 (4") squares. Cut each
  square in half diagonally to get
  8 M triangles.
- 6 (3¼") squares. Cut each
  square in quarters diagonally to
  get 23 A triangles (and 1 extra).
- 3 (2½") squares for block
  centers.
- 21 (1½"-wide) strips.

Planning Ahead
The Pineapple block is easy to
sew, but it takes planning to
achieve the overall design of this
quilt. Make one block at a time,
using the *Planning Diagram* at
right as a guide. Color placement is the critical factor to
make the snowflakes appear, so
be sure to check each block
against the diagram frequently
as you sew.

   Pin an identifying label on
each completed block so you'll
know how to lay them out later.

Foundation Piecing
Note: We used bright fabrics
and red thread for photography
to make steps more visual. Steps
were sewn on a half-block foundation, but steps are essentially
the same for all block types.

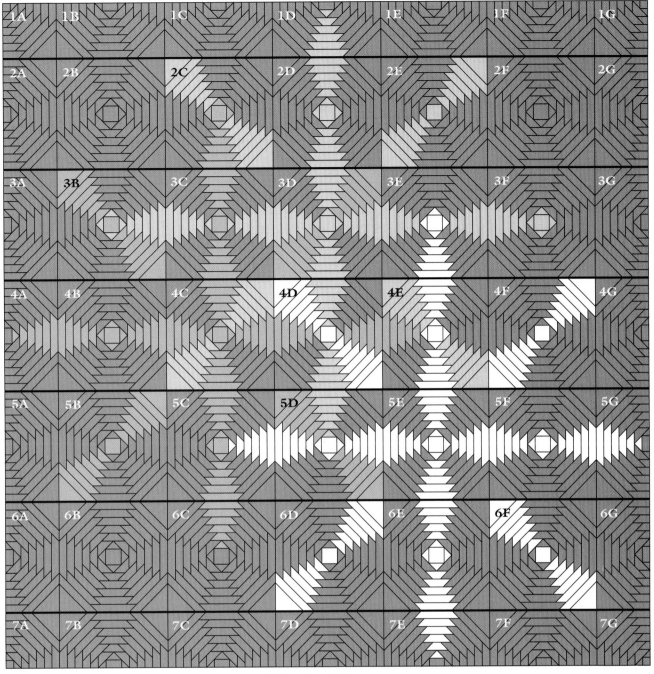

Planning Diagram

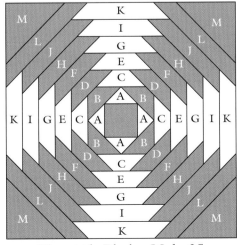

Pineapple Block—Make 25.

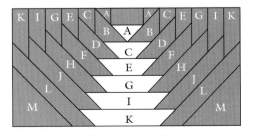

Half-Block—Make 20.

33

Foundation piecing takes a little getting used to, but it provides a sewing line that guarantees a nice finished block.

1. Trace quarter-block pattern (page 35) onto tracing paper.

2. Turn paper to align pattern with 1 side of traced square. Trace pattern again. Continue tracing pattern until all 4 corners are completed.

3. Draw a ¼" seam allowance around all sides of block. (We didn't do this for photography, and we were sorry later.) Cut out foundation paper on outside (seam allowance) lines.

4. Retrace or photocopy complete block to get 25 block foundations. In same manner, trace 20 (7" x 14") half-block foundations and 4 (7") square quarter-block foundations.

5. Start with half-block 2A. (Stitch 4 corner quarter-blocks last.) Pin a 1½" x 2½" piece on foundation center, letting seam allowances extend over edges of drawn block *(Photo A)*. On a full block, you'll pin a 2½" square at center as shown.

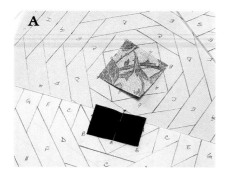

6. Pin an A triangle to 1 side of center square, right sides facing *(Photo B)*. On half-blocks and quarter-blocks, center each triangle on seam as shown—excess fabric is trimmed after block is complete. Set sewing

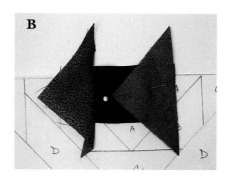

machine at 10–12 stitches per inch (tight stitches hold fabric firmly and perforate foundation closely for easy removal).

7. Turn foundation over to wrong side and stitch on drawn seam line *(Photo C)*. To secure stitches, backstitch at beginning and end of each seam.

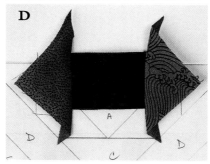

8. Clip threads. Turn foundation back to right side and press A triangles flat *(Photo D)*. Sew and press A triangle(s) to remaining side(s) of center piece in same manner.

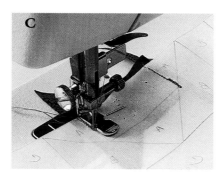

9. Choose a strip for first B segment. Pin it in place with right sides facing and matching raw edges *(Photo E)*. Stitch strip to block from wrong side as before

(Photo F). Press. Trim strip about ¼" from end of seam. Stitch remaining Bs in same manner, using different strips.

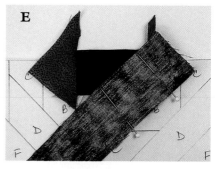

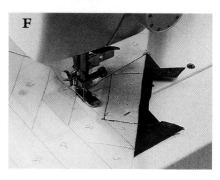

10. Stitch C strips in same manner *(Photo G)*. When all Cs are stitched, trim excess fabric from previous row, folding foundation paper out of the way *(Photo H)*.

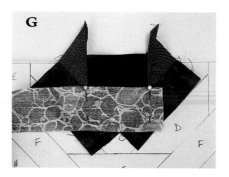

11. Stitch around block in same manner until block is complete, adding strips in alphabetical order. Be careful to leave seam allowance on all pieces on outside edges of each block.

12. Before you remove foundation paper, use a large square ruler to square up block and trim excess fabric on edges. Full blocks should be 14½" square, half-blocks should be 7½" x 14½", and quarter-blocks should be 7½" square.

13. Tear paper foundation away from completed block, being careful not to pull on stitching.

14. Make 25 blocks, 20 half-blocks, and 4 corner blocks as shown in *Planning Diagram*.

Quilt Top Assembly

1. Lay out blocks in 7 horizontal rows as shown in *Planning Diagram*. Check position of each block carefully.

2. When satisfied with placement, join blocks in rows. Then join rows to complete quilt top.

Quilting and Finishing

Quilt shown is machine-quilted with allover stippling. Quilt as desired.

Make straight-grain or bias binding to bind quilt edges.

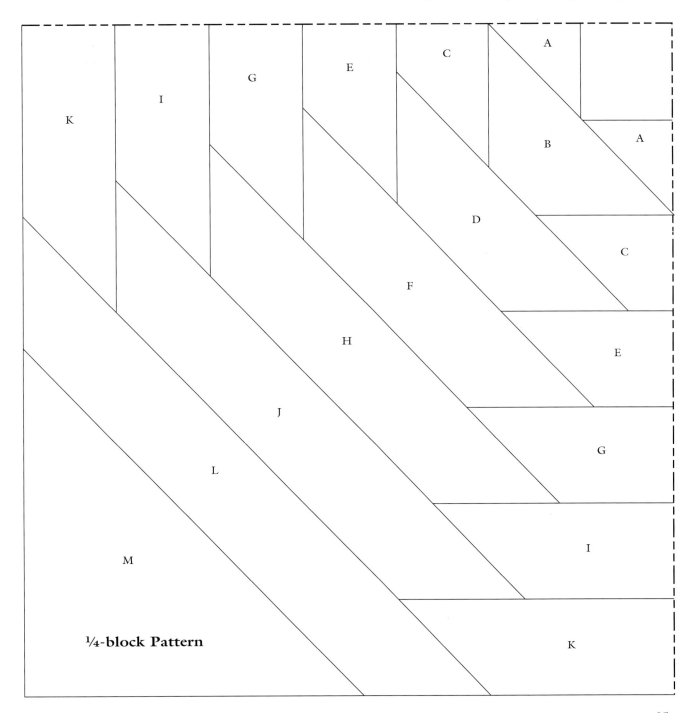

¼-block Pattern

Quilts Across America

Watermelon

Stars of Yesterday

Feathered Star

Winds of Time

Re-Vision

Kristi Hammer
Yuma, Arizona

Quilting is all in the family for Kristi Hammer. Her mother, sister, and brother are all quilters. "Quilting brings my family together and keeps us together," Kristi says.

The family quilters do a quilt retreat weekend twice a year. Far from the cares of children and husbands, Kristi's family rents a hotel conference room and sets up shop for three days. "We have tons of fun and share ideas," she says. "Quilting is so much a part of us, I can't imagine what my family life would be without quilting."

With such a quilting tradition, it wasn't hard for Kristi to get started as a quiltmaker. She completed her first quilt before high school. She enjoys an even earlier memory of her mother, Darlene Dommer, working with Aunt Merna and Grandma Jan to make a Trip Around the World quilt. "We had toilet tissue running the length of the floor" to indicate each row of the pattern, Kristi remembers. "I was too young to handle the fabrics, so I was the 'tape girl'," putting sewn segments in place on each strip of tissue.

"I can't imagine what my family life would be without quilting."

Now a new generation is starting to quilt. Kristi's husband, Dan, helps her baste. Their 5-year-old son, Zachary, is learning to cut and sew.

In addition to quilting with family, Kristi is a member of the Yuma Quilters.

Watermelon
1998

Strip piecing, set-in seams, appliqué, and yo-yos—*Watermelon* has it all.

Kristi Hammer strip-pieced the 48 star points of this quilt, using different values of pink and green fabrics. With lots of family advice, she arranged the units on her flannel board until she found a setting everybody liked.

When Kristi added the swag borders to the pieced top, the combination of graduated pinks and deep green looked like watermelon and rind, so that's the name she gave the quilt. Instead of black seeds, however, she added yo-yos with white pearl centers.

Watermelon won a blue ribbon at the 1999 Road to California quilt show.

Watermelon

Finished Size
Quilt: 69" x 69"
Blocks: 1 (27¾" x 27¾")

Materials*
2 fat quarters (18" x 22")
   pink-on-white prints
6 fat quarters assorted light pinks
17 (⅛-yard) pieces white,
   cream, light green, and
   light pink prints
9⅜" square *each* of 2 light
   yellow prints
2 (½-yard) pieces and 3 (⅜-yard)
   pieces medium pink prints
5 fat quarters medium-value
   cream/tan prints
6 (1⅝") strips medium prints
5 (⅜-yard) pieces dark green
   prints
1 fat quarter darkest green print
1 fat quarter dark red print
10 (1⅝") strips dark prints
¾ yard binding fabric
4½ yards backing fabric
28 (³⁄₁₆"-diameter) sew-on
   beads or pearls

*Note: These materials, and the
cutting list that follows, are a
suggestion for those who wish
to purchase fabrics for this quilt.

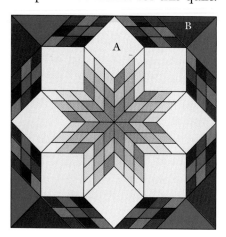

Star Block—Make 1.

If possible, we recommend that
you treat this project as a true
scrap quilt—select a palette of
scraps from your "stash" and cut
pieces individually as needed.

Pieces to Cut
Instructions are for rotary cutting and quick piecing. Appliqué
patterns D–M are on pages 44
and 45.
From each *pink-on-white print*
• 1 (12½") square. From this,
   cut 4 (6¼") A squares for
   center block.
• 1 (1⅝" x 15") strip.
• 11 (3½") C squares.
From lightest pink fat quarter
• 1 (9⅜") square. Cut square in
   quarters diagonally to get 4 B
   triangles.
• 1 (1⅝" x 15") strip.
• 6 (3½") C squares.
From each *remaining light pink
fat quarter*
• 5 (4½" x 10") pieces. From
   these, cut 5 of Pattern D.
• 1 of Pattern H. (You need a
   total of 4 Hs, but cut 1 from
   each fabric to have a choice of
   fabric combinations later.)
• 2 (1⅝" x 15") strips.
From all remaining light fabrics
• 3 (1⅝" x 15") strips.
• 172 (3½") C squares.
• 8 of Pattern L from light
   green scraps.
From each *½-yard medium pink*
• 4 (1⅜" x 42") strips for inner
   border.
From each *medium pink fabric*
• 5 (5½" x 10") pieces. From
   these, cut 5 of Pattern E.
• 1 (1⅝" x 15") strip.
• 1 of Pattern G.

From darkest cream/tan print
• 1 (12½") square. From this,
   cut 4 (6¼") A corner squares.
• 1 (1⅝" x 15") strip.
From each of 2 cream prints
• 1 (12½") square. From this,
   cut 4 (6¼") A squares.
• 1 (1⅝" x 15") strip.
• 11 (3½") C squares.
From each of 2 cream prints
• 1 (9⅜") square. Cut square in
   quarters diagonally to get 4 B
   triangles.
• 1 (1⅝" x 15") strip.
• 9 (3½") C squares.
From each *dark green fabric*
• 5 (6½" x 10") pieces. From
   these, cut 5 of Pattern F.
• 1 (1⅝" x 15") strip.
• 1 each of patterns J and K.
   (You need a total of 4 Js and
   4 Ks, but cut 1 from each fabric to have a choice of fabric
   combinations later.)
From darkest green print
• 1 (9⅜") square. Cut square in
   quarters diagonally to get 4 B
   triangles.
• 24 of Pattern M for yo-yos.
From dark red print
• 1 (9⅜") square. Cut square in
   quarters diagonally to get 4 B
   triangles.
• 4 of Pattern M for yo-yos.

Center Block Assembly
1. Sort out 16 (1⅝" x 15")
strips each of light, medium,
and dark values.
2. Join 3 light strips as shown
(*Diagram A*). Instead of matching ends of strips, offset each
strip about 1½" (this allows you
to get more cuts per strip set).
3. Lay strip set on cutting mat

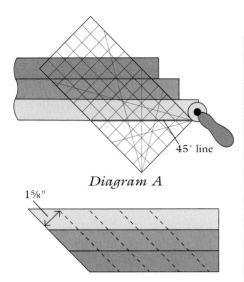

Diagram A

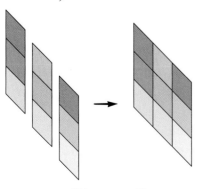

Diagram B

with uneven end at right (if you are left-handed, reverse directions throughout). Place ruler on strip set, aligning a 45°-angle line with bottom edge of strip set *(Diagram A)*. Trim uneven ends as shown.

4. Turn strip set upside down to continue cutting *(Diagram B)*. Measuring from trimmed edge, cut 4 (1⅝"-wide) diagonal segments.

5. Make a total of 4 light strip sets, 4 medium strip sets, and 4 dark strip sets. Cut all strip sets in same manner.

6. For each light star point, select 3 light segments. Join segments, offsetting adjacent segments to match seams correctly *(Diagram C)*. Assemble 48 diamonds, 16 each of light, medium, and dark fabrics.

Diagram C

❖QUILT SMART❖

Machine-Stitching a Set-In Y-Seam

When three seams come together in a Y-angle, use this technique to set the pieces together.

It's important to remember—**don't stitch into the seam allowance** as in most patchwork. Lightly mark the seam allowance on the wrong side of each piece so you won't stitch beyond that crucial matching point. (In diagrams, this point is indicated by a block dot.)

For this example, let's look at the star unit that consists of two diamonds and one square.

1. With right sides facing, match diamond to 1 side of square *(Diagram 1)*. With square on top, begin at ¼" seam line and sew 2 stitches forward and 2 stitches back. Take care not to sew into seam allowance. Then stitch to edge of fabric (no need to backstitch here because another seam will cross and hold this seam in place). Clip thread and take work out of sewing machine.

2. With right sides facing, match another diamond to adjacent side of square. With square on top, sew from outside edge *(Diagram 2)*. Backstitch at seam line.

3. With right sides facing, match points and edges of diamonds. Fold square out of the way. Beginning with a backstitch at inner seam line, sew to edge of fabric *(Diagram 3)*.

4. Press center seam open and square's seam allowances toward diamonds *(Diagram 4)*. Trim seam allowances even with unit edges.

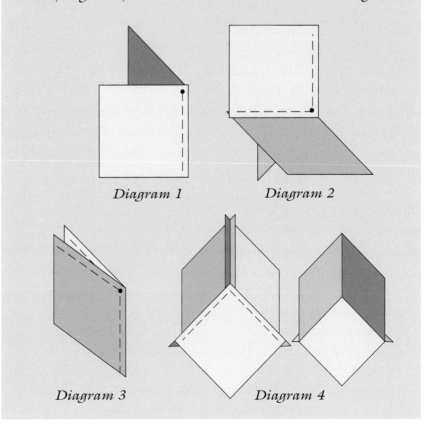

Diagram 1   *Diagram 2*

Diagram 3   *Diagram 4*

41

Block Assembly Diagram

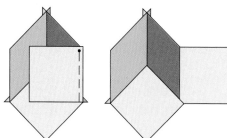

Diagram D

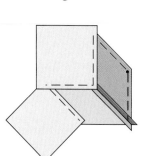

Diagram E

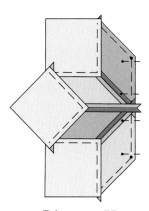

Diagram F

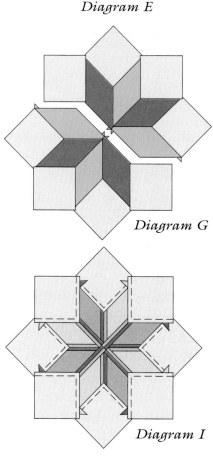

Diagram G

Diagram H

Diagram I

7. For center star, select 4 light diamonds and 4 medium diamonds. Lay out diamonds, alternating light and medium; then lay out A squares, positioning fabrics as shown (*Block Assembly Diagram*). See Quilt Smart, page 41, for instructions on setting squares into each pair of diamonds.

8. With right sides facing, place adjacent square on top of right diamond in each pair. Begin stitching at ¼" seam line and sew to raw edge (*Diagram D*). Make 4 units. Press seam allowances toward diamonds.

9. With right sides facing, match square of 1 unit with diamond of adjacent unit (*Diagram E*). With square on top, stitch from outside edge, ending with a backstitch at inner seam line (seam shown in red).

10. Align unstitched edges of diamonds, folding adjacent A square inside to keep it out of seam allowance. Pin-match diamonds. Begin sewing with a backstitch at inner seam line (*Diagram F*) and sew through all seams to edge of fabric. Press diamond seam allowances open and corner square seams toward center of block. Assemble 2

halves of star (*Diagram G*).

11. Join squares of each half to opposite diamond as described in Step 9.

12. Pin-match diamonds along length of center seam (*Diagram H*). Backstitch at top seam line and stitch precisely through center, ending with a backstitch at bottom seam line. Press seam allowance open. Press corner seam allowances toward diamonds (*Diagram I*).

13. Set-in 8 dark diamonds at each corner as shown (*Block Assembly Diagram*).

14. Join B triangles of dark red and darkest green in pairs as shown. Sew triangle units to each corner to complete block.

Quilt Top Assembly

1. Cut each yellow square in quarters diagonally to get 4 B triangles. Referring to photo, lay out remaining diamonds, A squares, and B triangles around center square.

2. Join diamond pairs as before. Set a square or triangle into each pair. Press.

3. Join adjacent units, setting in

42

each piece as needed until middle section is complete.

4. For inner border, select 1 set of strips for center of each border and 1 set for border corners. Cut corner strips in half. Join a corner strip to each end of center strips.

5. Measure length of quilt top through middle of pieced section. Trim 2 border strips to match length, measuring from center of strip. Sew borders to quilt sides. Press seam allowances toward borders. Measure width of quilt in same manner, including side borders. Trim and piece borders to quilt sides.

6. Choose 51 C squares for each side border. Join squares in 6 rows, with 17 squares in each row. Assemble 3 rows to make a single border unit for each side. Stitch borders to quilt sides.

7. Join remaining squares in 6 rows with 23 squares in each row. Assemble 3 rows to make a border unit for each remaining quilt side. Stitch borders to top and bottom edges of quilt.

8. See Quilt Smart at right for instructions on making yo-yos. Make 24 green yo-yos and 4 red yo-yos for appliquéd border.

9. Referring to photo, center 5 D/E/F swags on each quilt side, covering each end with a green yo-yo. Appliqué swags in place.

10. Position G, J, and K pieces at each corner as shown, tucking H and L pieces under larger pieces and placing a red yo-yo at top of each unit to cover ends. When satisfied with placement, appliqué corner pieces in place.

11. Stitch pearls into center of each yo-yo.

Quilting and Finishing

Quilt as desired. On quilt shown, Kristi Hammer machine-quilted different motifs in squares, triangles, and border.

Make bias or straight-grain binding from reserved fabric. Bind quilt edges.

❖QUILT SMART❖

Making Yo-Yos

1. Turn under seam allowance on edge of each circle (*Diagram 1*). Use matching thread to baste around circle, securing folded edges. Overlap first and last stitches.

2. Pull thread to gather circle tightly (*Diagram 2*). Secure end of thread with back-stitches or knot. Clip excess thread. Flatten gathered circle with gathers in center as shown.

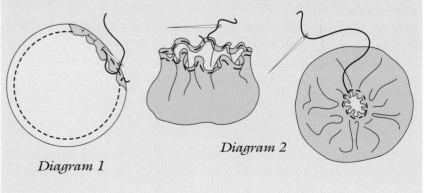

Diagram 1

Diagram 2

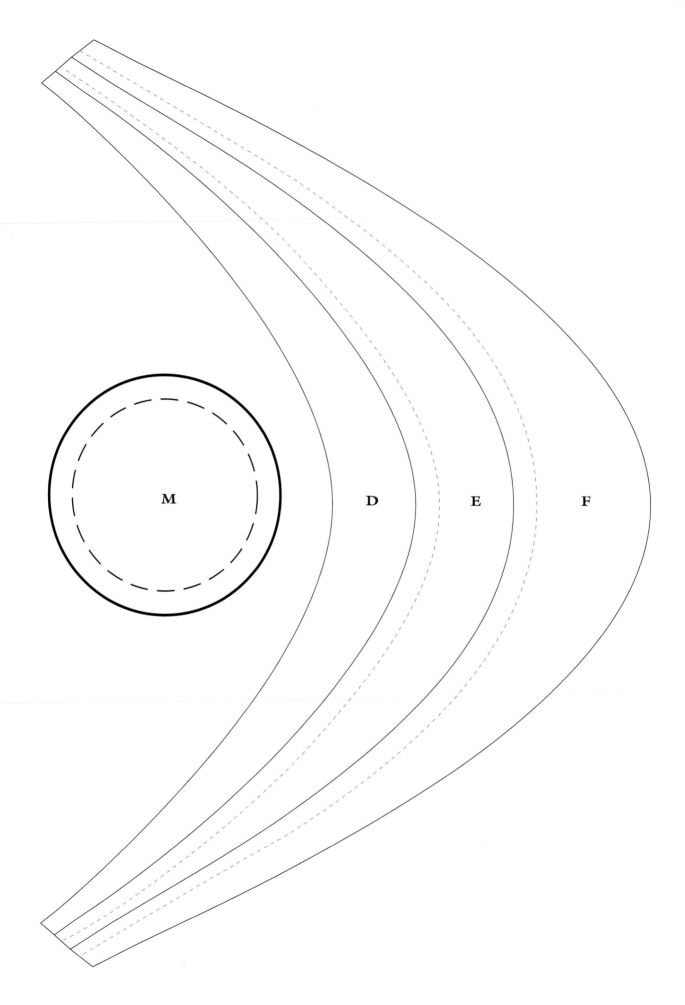

M

D

E

F

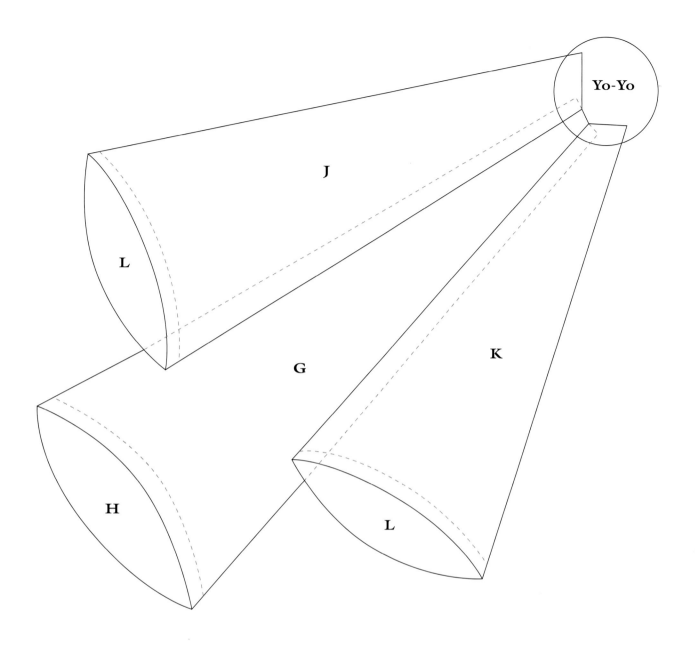

Yo-Yo

J

L

G

K

H

L

Mail-Order Resources

Quiltmaking supplies are available at craft and fabric stores, especially quilt specialty shops. Consult your telephone directory to find a shop in your area.

If you prefer to have supplies delivered to your door, you can order all kinds of fun things from a mail-order catalog. The following catalogs are excellent suppliers of fabric, notions, and other supplies. All have toll-free telephone numbers and will mail a catalog to you at no charge.

Connecting Threads
P.O. Box 8940
Vancouver, WA 98668
(800) 574-6454

Keepsake Quilting
P.O. Box 1618
Centre Harbor, NH 03226
(800) 865-9458

The Quilt Farm
P.O. Box 7877
St. Paul, MN 55107
(800) 435-6201

Stars of Yesterday

Inspired by an antique quilt, Kristi Hammer used reproduction fabrics to make these Union Star blocks. She changed the value placement in each block to make the piecing a challenge. Our instructions call for equal amounts of pink and brown (from pale pink and barely tan to almost-red and deep chocolate), but you can use any fabrics you like.

Finished Size
Quilt: 70" x 84"
Blocks: 20 (12" x 12")

Materials
14" x 22" piece *each* 10 pink prints and 10 brown prints (includes binding)
9" x 16" piece *each* 20 light shirting prints for block backgrounds
1¾ yards light tan for sashing
2⅛ yards border fabric
4¼ yards 45"-wide backing fabric or 2⅛ yards 90"-wide backing fabric

Pieces to Cut
Instructions are for rotary cutting and quick piecing. Cut all strips cross-grain except as noted. Cut pieces in order listed to get best use of yardage.
From each *pink and brown print*
- 1 (2½" x 22") strip for pieced binding.
- 1 (8") square for D triangle-squares.
- 3 (5¼") squares. Cut each square in quarters diagonally to get 12 B triangles.
- 1 (4½") A square.
- 4 (2½") C squares.

From each *background fabric*
- 1 (8") square for D triangle-squares.
- 1 (5¼") square. Cut square in quarters diagonally to get 4 B triangles.
- 4 (2½") C squares.

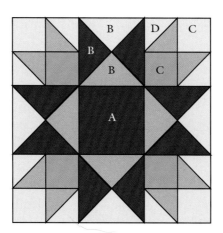

Union Square Block—Make 20.

From sashing fabric
- 6 (2½" x 60") lengthwise strips.
- 13 (2½" x 28") strips. From these, cut 25 (2½" x 12½") sashing strips.

From border fabric
- 4 (6½" x 75") lengthwise strips. Use remaining fabric for straight-grain binding, if desired.

Block Assembly
1. On wrong side of each 8" square of background fabric, mark a 2-square by 2-square grid of 2⅞" squares, leaving a 1" margin on all sides *(Diagram A)*. Draw diagonal lines through squares as shown.

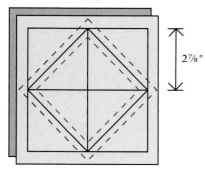

Diagram A

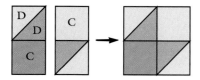

Diagram B

Diagram C

2. Match each marked piece with an 8" square of pink or brown fabric, right sides facing. Stitch ¼" seam on both sides of diagonal lines. (Red line on diagram shows first continuous stitching path; blue line shows second path.) Press. Cut on all drawn lines to get 8 D triangle-squares from each fabric pair.

3. For 1 block, select 4 Bs, 4 Cs, and 8 D triangle-squares, all with same background fabric. From pink and brown prints, choose 1 A square, 4 B triangles of 1 print and 8 Bs of another print, and 4 C squares.

4. For each corner unit, join a print C square, a background C square, and 2 D triangle-squares as shown *(Diagram B)*. Make 4 corner units. Press seam allowances toward Cs.

5. For each triangle unit, join B triangles in pairs as shown *(Diagram C)*. Press seam allowances toward same fabric in each pair. Join pairs to complete unit. Make 4 triangle units.

6. Lay out 4 corner units, 4 triangle units, and A square in 3 rows as shown *(Block Assembly Diagram)*. Position triangle units with background fabric at outside edge and corner units with background C square in outside corner.

7. Sew triangle units to opposite sides of A. Sew corner units to remaining triangle units as shown. Press seam allowances toward triangle units.

8. Join rows to complete block.

9. Make 20 blocks, varying fabrics and value placement as desired.

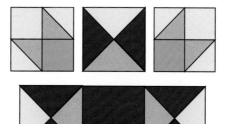

Block Assembly Diagram

Quilt Top Assembly

1. Referring to photo, lay out blocks in 5 horizontal rows with 4 blocks in each row. Lay 12½" sashing strips between blocks and at row ends. Move blocks around to get a nice balance of color and value.

2. When satisfied with block placement, join blocks and sashing strips in each row. Press seam allowances toward sashing.

3. Lay out rows again, placing 60" sashing strips between rows. Join rows and sashing, trimming sashing strips to fit.

Border

1. Measure length of quilt through middle of quilt top. Trim 2 border strips to match length. Stitch border strips to quilt sides, easing to fit as needed. Press seam allowances toward borders.

2. Measure width of quilt through middle and trim remaining borders to fit. Sew border strips to top and bottom edges of quilt, easing to fit.

Quilting and Finishing

1. Mark quilt top with desired quilting design. On quilt shown, blocks are outline-quilted. Create your own design for sashings and border, or look for commercial stencils to fit those areas.

2. Layer backing, batting, and quilt top. Baste. Quilt as desired.

3. For pieced binding as shown, sew 15 (2½" x 22") strips end-to-end to get 8¾ yards of continuous straight-grain binding. If you prefer, you can make continuous bias or straight-grain binding from a single fabric. Bind quilt edges.

Barbara Swinea
Fairview, North Carolina

*B*arbara Swinea laughs when she remembers the polyester leisure suits she used to make for her husband. They were a challenge, and that's the way Barbara likes her sewing projects—the more complicated they are, the better she likes them.

A lifelong sewer, Barbara didn't know anything about quilts except that her grandmother made some. When her grandmother gave her an unfinished quilt top, Barbara wondered, "What on earth am I supposed to do with it?" But once she learned how to finish it, she was hooked on quiltmaking.

"Accurate machine piecing and fine hand quilting are my constant goals."

"Accurate machine piecing and fine hand quilting are my constant goals," Barbara says. She creates prize-winning original quilts that reflect her fortitude in meeting a challenge.

When the Swineas lived in Florida in the 1970s, "I didn't know a single quilt-maker," Barbara says. But when they moved to North Carolina, she found a thriving community of quiltmakers. "I've made wonderful friends in quilting, and we go everywhere," she says. Barbara is a founding member of the Asheville Quilt Guild and has served two terms as president.

Feathered Star
1996

When Barbara Swinea decided she wanted to make a feathered star quilt, she had a vision in her head. But the finished quilt isn't at all like what she originally intended.

Barbara chose a block she liked and a palette of browns and naturals, using the backs of some fabrics to get more variety of tone.

"This quilt just evolved as I went along," Barbara says. "After I made the center part of the quilt, I drafted the rest on graph paper." The biggest challenge was deciding what to do next at each corner.

Feathered Star has won several prestigious awards for Barbara. It was Best of Show at the 1996 North Carolina

Quilt Symposium and at Silver Dollar City in 1997. The quilt also won blue ribbons at the American Quilter's Society show in Paducah, Kentucky, in 1997, at the 1998 Quilter's Heritage Celebration in Lancaster, Pennsylvania, and the Indiana Heritage Quilt show.

Feathered Star

Finished Size
Quilt: 75" x 82"
Blocks: 5 (18⅜" x 18⅜")

Materials
½ yard *each* 9 white and/or
  beige print fabrics*
⅜ yard *each* 5 brown print
  fabrics for stars*
⅜ yard *each* 10 brown print
  fabrics for pieced border*
2½ yards batik border fabric
  (includes fabric for binding)
1 yard binding fabric (optional)
5 yards backing fabric or
  2⅜ yards 90"-wide backing
* *Note:* Yardages are recommen-
dations. Use as many scrap
fabrics as desired, and cut equiv-
alent pieces as listed below.

Pieces to Cut
Note: See page 53 for optional
method for small triangle-
squares before cutting A pieces.

Instructions combine rotary
cutting and traditional cutting
with templates. (See Patterns B,
D, F, and N on page 54.) Cut
pieces in order listed to get best
use of yardage—largest pieces
are cut first. But if you're sure
you have enough scraps, you
can cut pieces as needed.

From all white/beige fabrics
- 11 (8⅜") squares. Cut each
  square in quarters diagonally
  to get 44 L triangles.
- 4 (6⅛" x 8⅝") pieces. With
  shorter sides as top and bottom, cut each rectangle in half
  diagonally from lower right
  corner to upper left to get 8
  H pieces.
- 2 (4⅜" x 8⅛") I pieces.

- 4 of Pattern N and 4 of
  Pattern N reversed.
- 34 (6¼") squares. Cut each
  square in half diagonally to
  get 68 G triangles.
- 2 (4¾") squares. Cut each
  square in half diagonally to
  get 4 K triangles.
- 4 (4⅜" x 5⅞") J pieces.
- 8 (4½") squares. Cut each
  square in half diagonally to
  get 16 M triangles.
- 20 of Pattern F.
- 20 (2¼") E squares.
- 60 (1½") C squares.
- 404 (1⅞") squares. Cut each
  square in half diagonally to
  get 808 A triangles.

From each brown fabric for stars
- 1 (1½"-wide) strip. From
  this, cut 8 (1½") C squares
  and 8 of Pattern B.

- 1 (8⅜"-wide) strip. From
  this, cut 1 (8⅜") square. Cut
  square in quarters diagonally
  for 4 L triangles (set aside for
  border). From remaining
  strip, cut 1 (6⅛") square for
  star center, 4 of Pattern D,
  and 4 of Pattern D reversed.
- 1 (1⅞"-wide) strip. From
  this, cut 24 (1⅞") squares.
  (Use scrap to cut last square if
  strip isn't quite long enough.)
  Cut squares in half diagonally
  to get 48 A triangles.

From remaining brown fabrics
- 10 (8⅜") squares. Cut each
  square in quarters diagonally
  to get 40 L triangles.
- 8 (5⅞" x 6¼") pieces. With
  shorter sides as top and bottom, cut each rectangle in
  half diagonally from lower left

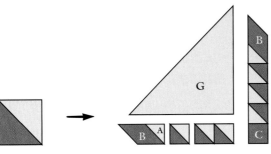
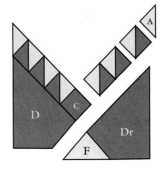
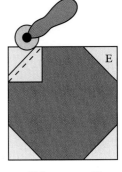

Diagram A   *Diagram B*   *Diagram C*

corner to upper right to get 16 Q pieces.

- 8 (6¼") squares. Cut each square in half diagonally to get 16 P triangles.
- 2 (5⅞") squares. Cut each square in half diagonally to get 4 R triangles.
- 252 (1⅞") squares. Cut each square in half diagonally to get 504 A triangles.
- 8 (1½" x 2") O pieces.
- 44 (1½") C squares.

From border fabric

- 4 (4" x 90") lengthwise strips for outer borders.
- 1 (2⅜" x 80") lengthwise strip. From this, cut 2 (2" x 40") lengths for side inner borders.
- 4 (2⅜" x 18") crosswise strips for corner inner borders.
- 1 (2" x 60") lengthwise strip. From this, cut 2 (2" x 30") lengths for top and bottom inner borders.

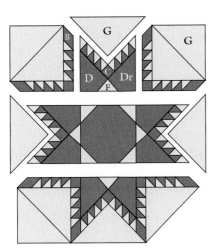

Block Assembly Diagram

Star Block Assembly

1. For each block, select 1 set of brown pieces. Use assorted light pieces as desired.

2. Sew each brown A triangle to a light A to make 48 triangle-squares. Join these into 16 rows, with 3 triangle-squares in each row *(Diagram A)*.

3. Sew a light A triangle to 1 leg of each B diamond.

4. For each block corner, select 2 triangle-square rows, 2 A/B units, 1 brown C square, and 1 G triangle. Sew an A/B unit to 1 end of each triangle-square row *(Diagram A)*. Sew 1 row to short leg of G. Add C to second row; then add row to adjacent leg of C to complete unit. Make 4 units for block.

5. For each block middle unit, select 2 triangle-square rows, 2 light A triangles, 1 brown C square, 1 F triangle, 1 D, and 1 D reversed *(Diagram B)*.

6. Sew an A triangle to dark end of each triangle-square row. Join C to light end of 1 row. Sew C row to D *(Diagram B)*. Then join second row to C square.

7. Join D reversed and F. Sew Dr/F to bottom of A/C/D to complete unit. Make 4 units for block.

8. See Quilt Smart on page 91 for tips on diagonal-corner quick-piecing technique. Following

those instructions, sew an E square to each corner of center square *(Diagram C)*.

9. Lay out units in 3 rows *(Block Assembly Diagram)*. Join units in each row; then join rows. Set-in a G triangle at each middle unit. Add G triangles at 3 corners to square off block (except for fourth corner).

10. Make 5 blocks. Referring to photo, decide which block will be in quilt center and add a G triangle to fourth corner of that block only.

Quilt Top Assembly

1. For top triangle unit *(Center Assembly Diagram)*, select 3 Gs, 2 each of H, J, and K, and an I. Join pieces in 3 rows as shown; then join rows to complete triangle unit. Repeat for bottom triangle unit.

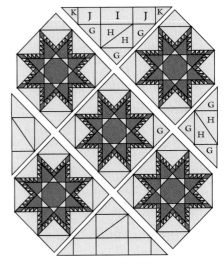

Center Assembly Diagram

2. For each side triangle unit, select 2 H pieces and 3 Gs. Join Hs as shown; then sew G triangles to both ends of rectangle. Add remaining G to complete triangle unit.

3. Lay out 5 blocks in X formation as shown and add triangle units. Join triangles and blocks in diagonal rows. Join rows to complete quilt center.

4. Sew top, bottom, and side inner borders to quilt center. Press seam allowances toward borders. Then add corner strips and miter corners.

Pieced Border

1. Join remaining light and dark A triangles to make 488 triangle-squares. You should have 16 dark A triangles left over.

2. Join 72 triangle-squares in 18 rows, with 4 triangle-squares in each row *(Top Border Assembly Diagram)*. You will have 8 triangle-squares left over for corner border.

3. For Row 1 of top border, select 5 dark L triangles, 4 light Ls, 5 light Cs, 4 dark Cs, 10 rows of triangle-squares, and 2 O pieces. Join units from left to right *(Top Border Assembly Diagram)*. Sew an O piece to end of 1 triangle-square row; then stitch row to dark L. Sew light C to dark end of another row

Quilt Assembly Diagram

and join this row to a light L. Join this to previous unit. Continue in this manner until row is complete as shown.

4. For Row 2 of top border, select 4 dark Ls, 3 light Ls, 4 light Cs, 3 dark Cs, 8 rows of triangle-squares, 2 M triangles, and 2 dark A triangles. Join an A to light end of 1 row; join row to a dark L triangle as shown. Sew M to opposite side

of triangle-square row. Working from left to right, assemble remaining units in same manner, to complete row.

5. Stitch Row 2 to bottom of Row 1. Sew combined border to top edge of quilt *(Quilt Assembly Diagram)*.

6. Repeat steps 3–5 to make bottom border. Sew border to bottom edge of quilt as shown.

7. Assemble both side borders in same manner, adding 1 light L and 1 dark L (with triangle-squares attached) to each row *(Quilt Assembly Diagram)*. Sew borders to quilt sides.

8. For Row 1 of corner border, select 3 dark Ls, 2 light Ls, 3 light Cs, 2 dark Cs, 6 rows of triangle-squares, and 2 dark A

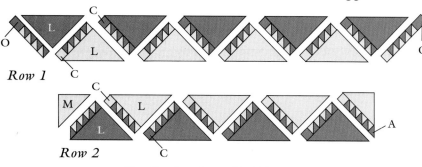

Top Border Assembly Diagram

triangles. Join units from left to right *(Corner Border Assembly Diagram)*. Sew a dark A to light end of 1 triangle-square row and a light C to other end; then stitch row to 1 M. Sew dark C to light end of another row and join this row to a dark L. Join units. Continue in this manner until row is complete as shown.

9. For Row 2 of corner border, select 2 dark Ls, 1 light L, 1 N, 1 N reversed, 2 light Cs, 1 dark C, 4 rows of triangle-squares, and 2 extra triangle-squares. Join units as shown.

10. Stitch Row 2 to bottom of Row 1. Make 4 corner borders.

11. Join P, Q, and R triangles in 3 rows as shown *(Corner Unit Assembly Diagram)*. Make 4 corner units. Sew each corner unit to top of Row 1 of each Corner Border. Points of P triangles extend slightly past border unit as shown.

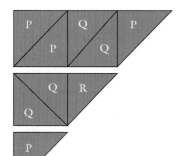

Row 1

Row 2

Corner Border Assembly Diagram

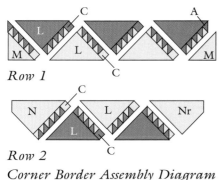

Corner Unit Assembly Diagram

12. Join combined corner units to each corner of quilt, aligning M and N pieces at each corner *(Quilt Assembly Diagram)*. Set-in all edges of each corner unit, adjusting seam allowance of inner border if necessary.

13. Sew outer borders to edges of quilt and miter corners.

Quilting and Finishing

Quilt as desired. Quilt shown has 1" cross-hatching stitched in light areas.

Make bias or straight-grain binding from reserved fabric. Bind quilt edges.

❖QUILT SMART❖

Helpful Aid for Piecing Small Triangle-Squares

Small triangles can be difficult to cut and handle, especially when there are as many as in *Feathered Star*. We found a product called Thangles helped improve sewing accuracy on these small pieces. Thangles, available for several sizes of triangle-squares, is a paper pattern that enables you to sew strips together in a manner that, when cut apart, gives you ready-made triangle-squares. For *Feathered Star*, you need Thangles for a 1" finished size.

Look for Thangles at your local quilt shop, or write to Thangles, P.O. Box 1010, Poolesville, MD 20837, or visit the internet site at www.thangles.com.

1. Instead of cutting 1⅞" squares from which A triangles are cut*, you'll need 1½"-wide strips of light and dark fabrics. Do not cut strips into squares.

2. Match 1 pair of strips, right sides facing. Pin Thangles pattern on top. Stitch on dashed lines.

3. Cut triangle-squares apart on solid lines. Tear paper away from seams, being careful to pull stitches as little as possible. Press triangle-squares open.

*Note: If you use Thangles, or a similar product, you still need to cut A triangles that are not made into triangle-squares. For these you need 1 (1⅞"-wide) dark strip and 2 (1⅞"-wide) light strips. Cut 8 (1⅞") dark squares; cut each square in half diagonally to get 16 A triangles for pieced border. Cut 40 squares from light strips and cut in half to get 80 A triangles for blocks.

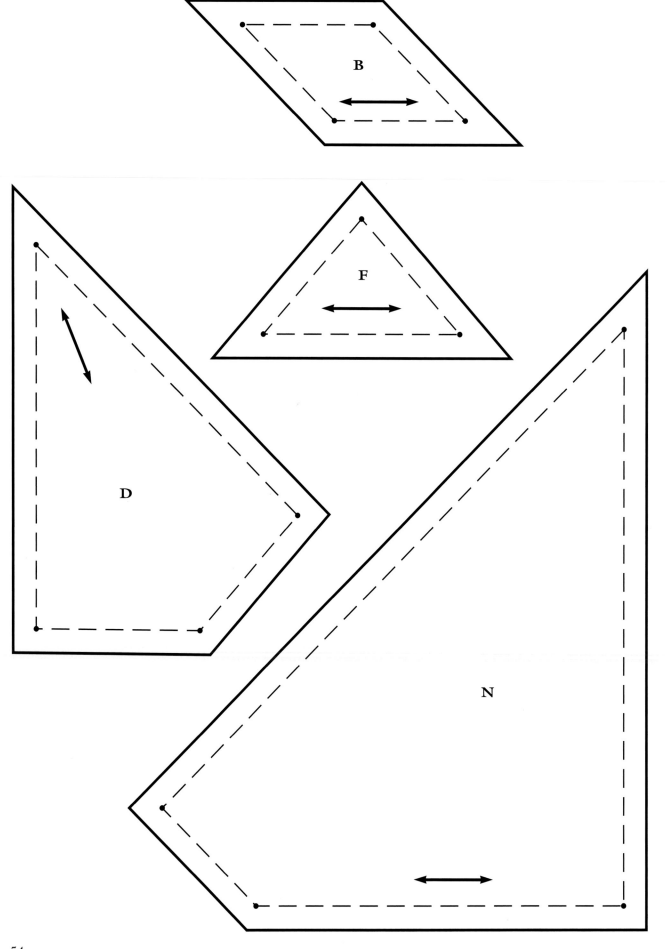

Terry Benzo
Pittsburgh, Pennsylvania

*I*t took Terry Benzo more than two years to complete her first quilt. But she made up for that slow start, creating more than 80 quilts and 68 wearables in the 15 years since then.

"My passion for quilting only increases with the years," says Terry. She likes scrap quilts and folk art-style quilts, but "my favorite is hand quilting—it's like the icing on the cake to me."

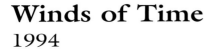

"My favorite is hand quilting—it's like the icing on the cake."

A long-time garment maker, Terry was introduced to quilting in a class at her local library. "Best class I ever took," she says, because of the impact quilting has had on her life. Terry still enjoys learning about quilting, trying out new ideas with traditional blocks.

And her work has improved, too. That first quilt had five stitches to the inch; today's work has three times as many per inch.

In addition to lecturing and teaching quiltmaking, Terry makes quilts and garments that appear in local and national quilt shows. A member of the Three Rivers Quilt Guild, Terry also belongs to a small bee because "quilting friends are a joy!"

Winds of Time
1994

When you're a true-blue, dyed-in-the-wool quiltmaker, just about anything in life is a good reason to make a quilt.

Terry Benzo planted bright flowers in her yard, hoping to attract butterflies. Lo and behold, it worked. On a warm day, watching colorful butterflies flit from flower to flower, she decided to capture the magic of her garden in a quilt so she could have butterflies even in the cold Pennsylvania winter.

Winds of Time combines piecing, appliqué, hand quilting, and fabric paint. Terry picked leaves in her neighborhood, dipped them in fabric paint, and lightly applied them to muslin. It looks like more, but there are only about eight types of leaves.

Winds of Time won a blue ribbon at the 1994 Three Rivers Quilt Show. It was also juried into the 1995 Quilters' Heritage Celebration in Lancaster, Pennsylvania.

Winds of Time

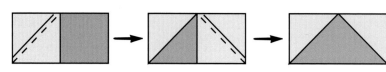

Diagram A

Finished Size
Quilt: 48¼" x 54¼"

Materials
2¾ yards muslin (includes backing fabric)

1½ yards plaid for outer border, vine, and leaves

⅛ yard light yellow

¼ yard *each* mottled brown and gray fabrics for flying geese

1 (1¾"-wide) strip *each* mottled yellow, light blue, green, and yellow-green for flying geese

51 (4") squares for butterflies

⅜"-wide bias pressing bar (optional)

8–10 leaves of various sizes and shapes

Fabric paint in assorted greens, blues, and red

Pieces to Cut
Cut all strips cross-grain except as noted.

From muslin
- 1 (35½"-wide) piece for center.
- 1 (56"-long) piece and 1 (15" x 56") piece for backing.
- 4 (2½" x 56") lengthwise strips for middle border.
- 10 (1¾" x 18") strips. From these, cut 132 (1¾") squares for flying geese units.

From border fabric
- 4 (3" x 54") lengthwise strips for outer border.
- 1 (21") square for bias vine.
- 60 leaves.

From light yellow
- 4 (1⅛"-wide) strips for inner border.

From mottled fabrics
- 132 (1¾" x 3") pieces for geese (at least 10 from each fabric).

From butterfly prints
- 51 butterflies.

Quilt Top Assembly
1. Lay muslin center flat, with newspapers or plastic protecting work surface. Coat 1 side of a leaf with paint. Blot excess paint on paper towel. Apply painted side of leaf to muslin to make a light impression. Repeat with as many leaves and paint colors as desired, filling in bottom and left side as shown. Let dry completely. Follow manufacturer's instructions to heat-set paint.

2. Appliqué butterflies on muslin as desired. Save a few to appliqué after borders are added.

3. Trim 2 yellow border strips to match length of muslin. Sew border strips to muslin sides. Press seam allowances toward borders. Trim remaining yellow strips to match width, including side borders. Sew strips to top and bottom edges of quilt.

4. See page 91 for Quilt Smart instructions for diagonal-corner quick-piecing technique. Using those instructions, sew 1¾" squares to corners of each 1¾" x 3" rectangle *(Diagram A)*.

5. Referring to photo, lay out flying geese around quilt center, arranging colors as desired. Pick 33 units for each side border and 33 units each for top and bottom borders. When satisfied with color placement, join geese in each row. Stitch side borders to quilt; then join top and bottom borders as shown.

6. Sew muslin borders to quilt, mitering corners. Add plaid borders in same manner.

7. See page 144 for tips on making continuous bias. Make 6¾ yards of 1⅛"-wide continuous bias from 21" square of border fabric.

8. Fold sides of bias strip over each other and press to make ⅜"-wide bias (use pressing bar if desired).

9. Starting at center of any side, pin bias onto muslin border, making gentle curves spaced about 5½" apart. Fold fabric under where ends of bias meet.

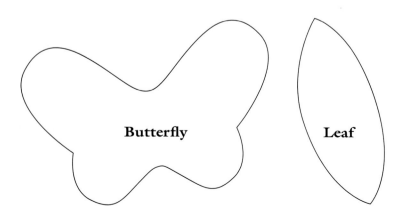

Butterfly

Leaf

Prepare leaves for appliqué and pin a leaf against vine inside each curve. When satisfied with placement, appliqué vine and leaves in place.

10. Appliqué remaining butterflies as desired.

Quilting and Finishing

Outline-quilt appliqués, painted leaves, and flying geese. On quilt shown, veins of each leaf are quilted. Terry Benzo quilted random swirls in background to represent breeze and bulrushes in quilt center. Pattern for bulrushes is on page 59.

Turn under ¼" on outer edge of plaid border and press. Turn folded edge to back of quilt and hem.

**Bulrush
Quilting Pattern**

Linda M. Anderson
Fresno, California

Way back in the 1970s, when wide-spread interest in quiltmaking was reborn, Linda Anderson joined her mother and sister in attempting to make their first quilt. "We didn't know what we were doing," Linda remembers. "We used polyester double-knit for the sashing and backing of our first quilt."

The Anderson women perservered and now all three are accomplished and productive quiltmakers. After taking many classes to improve her skills, Linda now does some teaching herself.

Quilting is Linda's main pleasure. She is a Department of Justice attorney who represents the United States and its agencies in civil litigation in the Eastern District of California, and her job creates a lot of tension. "When I get home, a little handwork drains all the negative energy right out of me," Linda says. "Quilting lets me live in my artistic side, in my own world of shape and color."

Linda is a member of the San Joaquin Valley Quilters Guild in the Fresno area, but she often makes the four-hour drive to Ridgecrest, California, for family and business, so she also belongs to the High Desert Quilt Guild of Ridgecrest.

"A little handwork drains all the negative energy right out of me."

Re-Vision
1998

For Linda Anderson, the first step in making a quilt is "think of someone you love." She made *Re-Vision* in memory of her grandmother, Theresa Dushane.

Mrs. Dushane made a lifetime of quilts for Lutheran missions, often using rectangular scraps to make unconventional nine-patch designs with no background fabric.

The reproduction fabrics Linda used to make *Re-Vision* were part of an award she received at the 1997 Road to California quilt show. (The prize-winning quilt, shown in Linda's photo above, was made in honor of her other grandmother, Ellen Anderson).

Linda alternated Double Nine-patch blocks with a "hollow block" that she

designed to use Grandma Dushane's favorite shape, the rectangle. An inner border of rectangles has no background fabric and is tied instead of quilted in tribute to Mrs. Dushane's quilts.

Re-Vision was juried into the Road to California quilt show in January 1999.

Re-Vision

Finished Size
Quilt: 83" x 83"
Blocks: 41 (9" x 9")

Materials
¼ yard each of 25 print fabrics
5½ yards white or muslin
2½ yards 90"-wide backing

Pieces to Cut
Instructions are for rotary cutting and quick piecing. Cut all strips cross-grain except border strips as noted. Cut pieces in order listed to get best use of yardage.

From each scrap fabric
- 2 (1½"-wide) strips. From these, cut 5 (1½" x 8") pieces for strip sets 1 and 2, 3 (1½" x 11") pieces for Strip Set 4, and 5 (1½" x 2½") F pieces.
- 1 (3½"-wide) strip. From this, cut 1 (3½" x 13") piece for Strip Set 3, 9 (3") squares for prairie points, and 2 (1½" x 2½") F pieces. Seven F pieces are extras.

From all remaining scrap fabrics
- 1 (1½"-wide) strip from each of 9 fabrics. From each of these, cut 3 (1½" x 11") pieces for Strip Set 4.

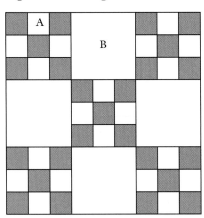

Block 1—Make 25.

- 4 (2⅜") squares from each of 4 fabrics. Cut each square in half diagonally to get 8 Z triangles of each fabric for Pinwheel blocks.

From white
- 1 (2⅜-yard) length. From this, cut 4 (6" x 85") lengthwise strips for borders. From remainder, cut 100 (1½" x 8") pieces for strip sets 1 and 2.
- 9 (3½"-wide) strips. From these, cut 100 (3½") B squares.
- 2 (5½"-wide) strips. From these, cut 16 (5½") C squares.
- 25 (1½"-wide) strips. From these, cut 32 (1½" x 10½") G strips, 32 (1½" x 9½") E strips, 32 (1½" x 7½") D strips, and 4 (1½" x 12½") H strips.
- 4 (11") squares. Cut each square in quarters diagonally to get 16 X setting triangles.
- 2 (7⅜") squares. Cut each square in half diagonally to get 4 Y corner triangles.

Block 1 Assembly
1. Stitch a 1½" x 8" white strip between 2 strips of same print fabric to make Strip Set 1 *(Strip Set 1 Diagram)*. Make 2 of Strip

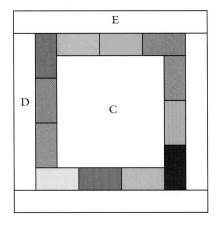

Block 2—Make 16.

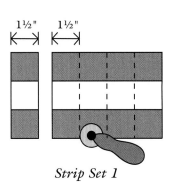

Strip Set 1

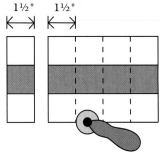

Strip Set 2

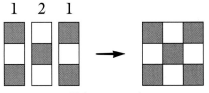

Diagram A

Set 1. Then stitch 1 strip of same print fabric between 2 white strips to make 1 of Strip Set 2 *(Strip Set 2 Diagram)*. Press all seam allowances toward print fabric.

2. Cut 5 (1½"-wide) segments from each strip set.

3. Join 2 segments of Strip Set 1 and 1 segment of Strip Set 2 to make a nine-patch unit *(Diagram A)*. Using all cut segments, you can make 5 nine-patch units of same fabric combination.

4. Repeat with remaining 1½" x 8" strips to get a total of 125 nine-patch units.

5. For each block, select 5 assorted nine-patches and 4 B squares. Join squares in horizontal rows *(Block Diagram)*. Join rows to complete block.

6. Make 25 of Block 1.

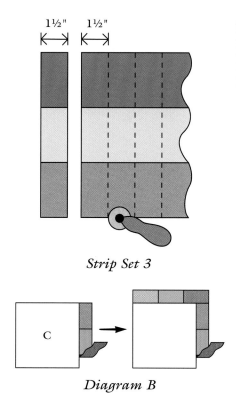

1½" 1½"

Strip Set 3

C

Diagram B

Block 2 Assembly

1. Join any 3 (3½" x 13") strips *(Strip Set 3 Diagram)*. Make 8 of Strip Set 3, varying fabrics. You will have 1 (3½" x 13") strip left over.

2. From each strip set, cut 8 (1½"-wide) segments to get a total of 64 segments, 4 for each block.

3. Match 1 segment to a C square, right sides facing and aligning top of segment with corner of square. Stitch segment to square, stopping at least 2" from corner of square, leaving end of segment unsewn *(Diagram B)*. Press seam allowances toward colored strip.

4. Sew second segment to top edge of combined units as shown. Press seam allowances toward print fabrics. Add third and fourth segments in same manner. Then go back and finish first seam, stitching over last segment.

5. Sew D strips to 2 sides of block.

Press seam allowances toward Ds. Then stitch E strips to remaining sides to complete block.

6. Make 16 of Block 2.

Side & Corner Blocks Assembly

1. For each side block, select 1 X triangle, 9 F pieces, and 2 Gs. Join 4 Fs in a row; then stitch row to 1 side of triangle *(Side Block Diagram)*. Press seam

allowances toward pieced row. Join remaining 5 Fs in a row and stitch row to second side of triangle. Last brick in each row extends past triangle; these are trimmed later.

2. Sew 1 G strip to triangle side as shown. Press seam allowance toward pieced row. Stitch second G to adjacent side in same manner to complete block.

3. Make 16 side blocks.

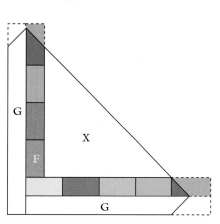

Side Block—Make 16.

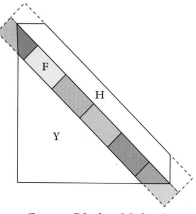

Corner Block—Make 4.

4. For corner block, select 1 Y triangle, 6 F pieces, and 1 H strip. Join Fs in a row *(Corner Block Diagram);* then sew row to diagonal edge of Y triangle. Handle triangle carefully as this edge is bias and can stretch if you're not careful. Add H to pieced row as shown. Press seam allowances toward pieced row. Make 4 corner blocks.

Quilt Top Assembly

1. Lay out blocks in 9 diagonal rows as shown *(Quilt Assembly Diagram).* Start and end each row with Block 1 and alternate blocks as shown. When satisfied with block placement, join blocks in each row.

2. Add side blocks to row ends as shown.

3. Join rows, mitering seams where side blocks meet.

4. Add corner blocks at each corner of quilt.

5. Trim ends of pieced strips even with X and Y triangles.

Borders

1. Select 2 (1½" x 11") strips of same print fabric and 1 strip of another fabric. Join strips as shown *(Strip Set 4 Diagram).* Press all seam allowances toward top strip. Make 34 of Strip Set 4.

2. Cut 4 (2½"-wide) segments from each strip set to get a total of 136 segments for border.

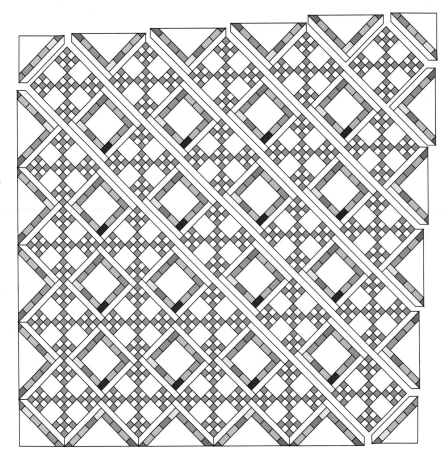

Quilt Assembly Diagram

3. Referring to photo, join 34 segments in a vertical row for each side border. Turn adjacent segments to offset seam allowances. Stitch rows to quilt sides, easing to fit as needed.

4. Join 2 horizontal rows with 34 segments in each row. Set aside.

5. For each Pinwheel block, select 4 Z triangles each of 2 fabrics. Join pairs of contrasting triangles to make 4 triangle-squares. Join squares in rows; then join rows to complete block *(Pinwheel Block Diagram).* Make 2 Pinwheel blocks with same fabric combination; then make 2 more blocks of second fabric combination.

6. Stitch Pinwheel blocks to both ends of each pieced border. Stitch borders to top and

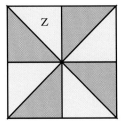

Pinwheel Block—Make 4.

bottom edges of quilt, easing to fit as needed.

7. Measure length of quilt through center of quilt top. Trim 2 white border strips to match length. Stitch border strips to quilt sides. Press seam allowances toward borders.

8. Measure width of quilt through center of quilt top, including side borders. Trim remaining white borders to match quilt width. Sew borders to top and bottom edges of quilt, easing to fit as needed.

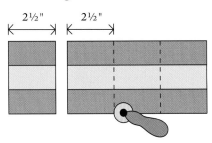

Strip Set 4

Quilting and Finishing

1. Mark quilt top with desired quilting design. Blocks of quilt shown are machine-quilted in-the-ditch and other areas of quilt are utility-quilted by hand. Pattern for heart-and-wave motif stitched in X triangles is at right. Same heart is quilted in each B square, and wavy lines in D, E, G, and H strips as well as white border. Linda also added tying in pieced border because her grandmother usually tied her quilts.

2. Layer backing, batting, and quilt top. Baste. Quilt as desired.

3. Fold 56 (3") squares in half *(Diagram C)* and in half again *(Diagram D)*. Press. Pin prairie points to 1 side edge of quilt top, aligning raw edges and overlapping points as needed to fit edge of quilt *(Diagram E)*. Baste. Repeat on each remaining side.

4. Fold backing of quilt away from edges; pin or baste to hold backing temporarily in place. Using a ¼" seam, stitch around edges of quilt through prairie points, quilt top, and batting.

5. Trim batting close to stitching. Press prairie points out. Remove pins or basting from backing. Turn under ¼" on each edge of backing and slip-stitch backing in place behind prairie points.

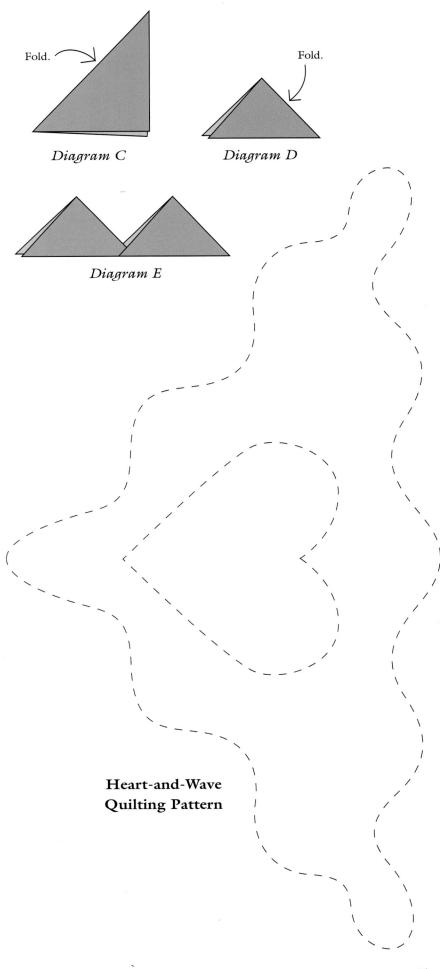

Fold.   *Diagram C*

Fold.   *Diagram D*

Diagram E

**Heart-and-Wave
Quilting Pattern**

Traditions in Quilting

Caroline Weber Pyne
Oxnard, California

Appliqué goes everywhere with Caroline Weber Pyne. At ball games, soccer practice, and waiting in carpool lines, this busy mom puts time to good use and sews. "It's *amazing* how much time is wasted waiting," Caroline says. "I'd rather accomplish something."

Caroline made her first quilt 20 years ago, but it isn't finished yet. She really started making quilts in 1993 after a visit to Ohio Amish country, where she saw a quilt in a store and said, "I can make that!" Her enthusiasm got a boost when she found she could take classes at a quilt shop just 10 minutes from home.

"I love taking classes," says Caroline, who counts Roberta Horton as a favorite teacher. "I love pushing myself to do daring things. I'm constantly being inspired and challenged, so quilting is always new."

"I love pushing myself to do daring things."

Caroline is a member of the Valley Quiltermakers Guild, the Camarillo Quilters Association, and a small group called Hanging by a Thread.

Victorian Rose
1997

Flipping through a book of Victorian tile designs, Caroline Pyne found one that caught her quiltmaker's imagination. She adapted it for appliqué and got to work.

Her first idea called for 15 blocks. But she found the design more interesting set on point, so she needed more blocks. When Caroline had made and joined 25 blocks, her quilt guild friends made

suggestions for the border.

Caroline says this quilt "practically made itself. When that happens, I know I have a winner."

Victorian Rose is indeed a winner, taking a judge's choice ribbon at the 1999 Road to California show. It also won second place at Valley Quiltmakers' 1997 show and was juried into the 1998 American Quilter's Society show.

Victorian Rose

Finished Size
Quilt: 94" x 94"
Blocks: 25 (13" x 13")

Materials
7½ yards printed muslin
3 yards green
1½ yards leaf print (includes binding)
1⅛ yards rose
1⅛ yards yellow
1 yard red tone-on-tone
½ yard brown print
8½ yards backing fabric

Pieces to Cut
Cut all strips cross-grain except as noted. Cut pieces in order listed to make best use of yardage. Make templates of patterns on pages 72 and 73.

From muslin
• 4 (4" x 99") lengthwise strips for border.
• 25 (13½") squares.
• 22 (3½"-wide) strips. From these, cut 60 (3½" x 13½") sashing strips and 24 (3½") sashing squares.
• 3 (15½") squares. Cut these squares in quarters diagonally to get 12 setting triangles.

Victorian Rose Block—Make 25.

• 2 (10⅛") squares. Cut these squares in half diagonally to get 4 corner setting triangles.

From green
• 3 (4"-wide) strips. From these, cut 25 of Pattern A.
• 23 (3"-wide) strips. From these, cut 32 of Pattern G and 72 of Pattern I.
• 48 of Pattern H.
• 4 of Pattern B.

From leaf print
• 32" square for binding.
• 200 of Pattern E.
• 40 of Pattern H.

From rose
• 200 of Pattern D.
• 40 of Pattern B.

From yellow
• 100 of Pattern F.
• 4 of Pattern H.

From red
• 100 of Pattern C.
• 100 of Pattern C reversed.

From brown print
• 100 of Pattern B.

Quilt Top Assembly
1. Fold 25 background squares in half crosswise, lengthwise, and diagonally *(Diagram A)*. Crease folds to make placement guides for appliqué.
2. Center piece A on a 13½" muslin square, aligning points

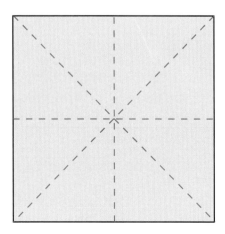

Diagram A

with diagonal placement lines *(Block Diagram)*. Using pattern on page 73 for placement, pin 4 brown print Bs, 4 Cs, 4 Cs reversed, 8 Ds, 8 Es, and 4 Fs in place. Tip of piece F should align with diagonal placement line about 7½" from center of block and Bs should be centered over horizontal and vertical guidelines.

3. When satisfied with position of all pieces, appliqué pieces in place on background fabric.

4. Make 25 blocks.

5. Lay out blocks in 7 diagonal rows as shown, alternating appliquéd blocks and sashing strips *(Quilt Assembly Diagram)*. End rows with setting triangles, being sure to match straight edges and corners of triangles as shown. (Don't worry that triangles are shorter than sashing strips—strips will be trimmed after borders are added.)

6. Between block rows, lay out sashing strips and sashing squares in rows as shown.

7. When satisfied with placement of all units, join blocks, sashing strips, and squares in each row. Press all seam allowances toward sashing strips.

8. Join rows to complete quilt center. Sew corner triangles in place as shown.

9. Referring to photo, center a rose B circle on each sashing square; then pin a leaf print H circle on top of it. Position 2 I pieces on each sashing strip, with a green H between them. Tuck I ends under adjacent circles. When satisfied with placement, appliqué pieces in place.

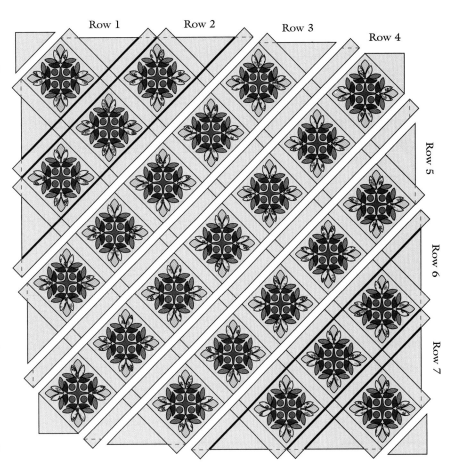

Quilt Assembly Diagram

Borders

1. Sew a muslin border strip to each edge of quilt; then miter corners. Press seam allowances toward borders.

2. At each border corner, center a green B circle; then pin a yellow H on top of it.

3. Fold quilt top in half to find middle of each border. Center green H circles on borders at middle points.

4. Referring to photo, position 4 Gs between each corner B and middle Hs. Cover ends of each G with a green H or rose B circle as shown. Pin leaf print Hs on top of each rose circle. When satisfied with placement, appliqué border pieces in place.

Quilting and Finishing

Outline-quilt around appliqués. On quilt shown, Caroline Pyne quilted half of appliqué motif in each setting triangle, using colored thread to match colors of appliqué. Corner triangles have quarter of design. (For tips on making your own quilting stencil, see page 99.) She filled background spaces with cross-hatched lines spaced 1" apart.

Make bias or straight-grain binding from reserved leaf print fabric. Bind quilt edges.

❖QUILT SMART❖

Make a Signature Patch

It's important to sign and date your quilt for posterity. Most antique quilts offer few clues about their origin, leaving empty pages where there could be history about women and family. Carolyn Miller is one quiltmaker who believes we owe it to future generations to leave a record of our quilts and who made them.

Incorporating a name or a date in the quilting is a time-honored method, as is embroidering these details on the quilt top or backing. The Quilters Guild of Indianapolis included a date in the appliqué (see page 114) and listed the name of the quiltmakers on the back.

Carolyn appliquéd a tree on the back of *Tie A Yellow Ribbon* (pictured on page 100), adding an embroidered ribbon (see photo at right) and a handwritten identification.

A practical label is a piece of fabric, hemmed on all sides, on which you embroider or write the desired information. For writing, use a fine-tipped permanent pen. Press freezer paper to the back of the fabric to stabilize it for writing. Peel off the freezer paper when the writing is complete and handstitch the label to the quilt back.

I

½ G

Place on fold.

H   B

72

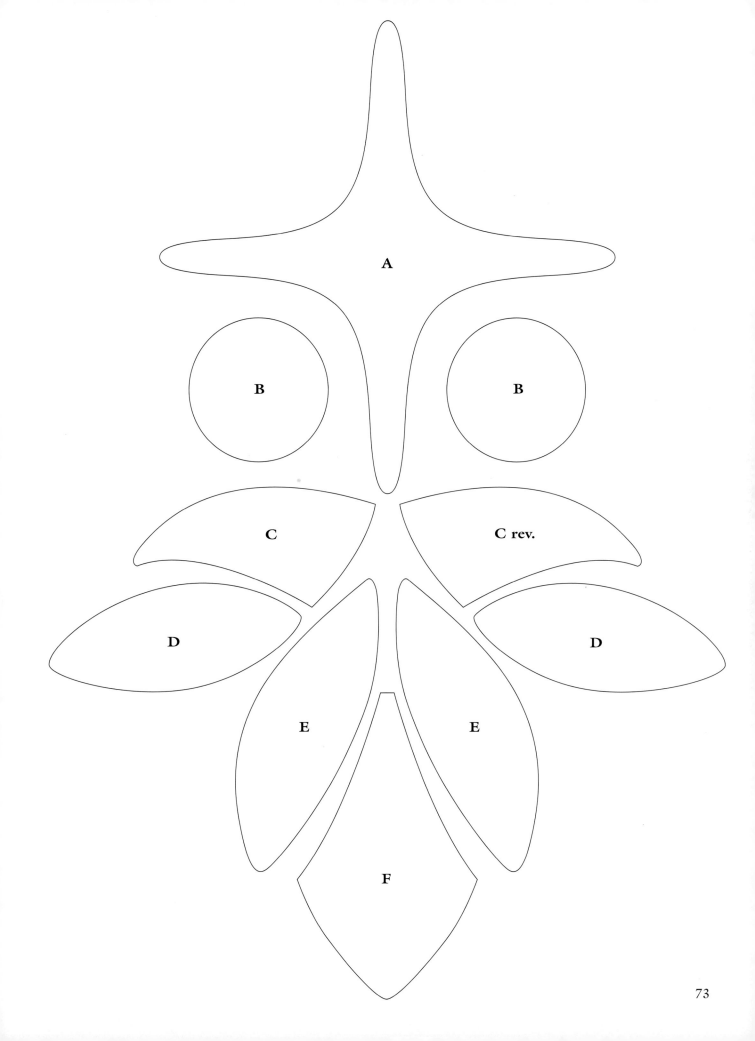

A

B   B

C   C rev.

D   D

E   E

F

Kathleen Moorhead Johnson
Alexander, North Dakota

*H*er sewing machine is one of Kathleen Johnson's best friends. Most of her other friends are quilters, too.

"I especially enjoy machine appliqué and quilting," says Kathleen. She hones her skills by taking classes, including some from author and machine-quilting expert Harriet Hargrave, whom Kathleen considers a mentor. "There's always something new to learn in this great world of quilting," she says.

In fact, it was a class that got Kathleen started in quilting. She was a mother with two pre-school children when she moved to a new town in 1983, and Kathleen thought taking a class could be a way to meet people and make new friends. The quilting class she chose turned out to be a fateful choice because it started Kathleen's love affair with quilts, quiltmakers, and her sewing machine.

"The love and support of other quilters is one of the best things to come out of learning to quilt."

Now Kathleen teaches quiltmaking herself. "I love to see my pupils succeed," she says. But it's friendship that Kathleen finds most important. She says, "The love and support of other quilters is one of the best things to come out of learning to quilt."

Kathleen is active in several area quilt groups, including the Dakota Prairie Quilters of Williston, the Prairie Rose Quilters of Watford City, the Prairie Quilters of Minot, the Badlands Quilt Guild, and the Quilters Guild of North Dakota, Fargo.

Autumn Splendor
1996

Kathleen Johnson knows how to get the most out of her sewing machine, a new Bernina 170E. With computerized stitches and other nifty features, it's a machine our grandmothers wouldn't have thought possible.

"It's wonderful to have machine-done pieces that look like handwork," says Kathleen. *Autumn Splendor* is one of Kathleen's machine-made quilts that pay homage to the merits of tradition.

Kathleen adapted the classic Oak Leaf design so she could use her machine's neat, even buttonhole-stitch for machine-appliqué. Using leaf prints in autumn colors, she achieved an elegant look without investing the time needed for handwork.

Autumn Splendor won a blue ribbon for Best Design Interpretation at the North Dakota State Fair. It was also juried into the 1997 American Quilter's Society show in Paducah, Kentucky.

Autumn Splendor

Finished Size

Quilt: 90" x 111"
Blocks: 12 (18" x 18")
        38 (6" x 6")
        8 (9" x 9")

Materials

7 yards tan
12 (½-yard) pieces leaf prints
1 yard binding fabric
3¼ yards 104"-wide backing

Pieces to Cut

Instructions are for rotary cutting, quick piecing, and traditional appliqué. Appliqué patterns are on page 79.

Cut strips cross-grain except as noted. Cut pieces in order listed for most efficient use of yardage.

From each *leaf print*

• 1 (9" x 21") piece. From this, cut 1 of Pattern A and 4 of Pattern B for appliqué.

From remaining leaf prints

• 8 (6" x 17") pieces, 1 for each 9" Maple Leaf block. From each of these, cut 1 (6" x 10") piece for F triangle-squares, 1 (3½" x 6½") E piece, 1 (3½") D square, and 1 (1" x 5") C piece. Keep each set together until needed for blocks.

• 19 (8" x 16") pieces for 6" Maple Leaf blocks. From each of these, cut 1 (7½") square for J triangle-squares, 2 (2½" x 4½") I pieces, 2 (2½") H squares, and 2 (1" x 3½") G pieces. Each set makes 2 small Maple Leaf blocks.

• Cut remaining fabric into 2⅝"-wide strips. From these, cut 206 (2⅝") M squares.

Oak Leaf Block—Make 12.

From tan

• Set aside 1⅛ yards for borders.

• 12 (18½") squares for Oak Leaf blocks. You should have 24½" x 111" left from this cut. Use this for next 3 cutting requirements.

• 5 (2⅜" x 24½") strips. From these, cut 42 (2⅜") squares. Cut each square in half diagonally to get 84 L triangles for sashing.

• 19 (4¼" x 24½") strips. From these, cut 93 (4¼") squares. Cut each square in quarters diagonally to get 370 K triangles for sashing (and 2 extra).

• 5 (3½" x 24½") strips. From these, cut 16 (3½") D squares and 4 (3½" x 9½") Q pieces.

• 5 (2½"-wide) strips. From these, cut 76 (2½") H squares.

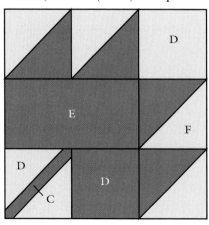

9" Maple Leaf Block—Make 8.

• 2 (6"-wide) strips. From these, cut 8 (6" x 10") pieces for F triangle-squares.

• 4 (7½"-wide) strips. From these, cut 19 (7½") squares for J triangle-squares.

• 4 (6½"-wide) strips. From these, cut 22 (3½" x 6½") P pieces and 32 (2" x 6½") N pieces for borders.

• 1 (9½"-wide) strip. From this and scraps, cut 24 (2" x 9½") O spacer strips for borders.

Block Assembly

1. Fold each background square in half diagonally (*Diagram A*). Crease folds to make placement guides for appliqué.

2. Center piece A on each block (*Block Diagram*) and pin. Pin 4 Bs in place, aligning stems with diagonal placement guides and tucking stem ends under A. When satisfied with placement, appliqué A and Bs in place. Complete 12 Oak Leaf blocks.

3. On wrong side of each tan 6" x 10" piece, mark 2 (3⅞") squares, leaving a 1" margin (*Diagram B*). Draw diagonal lines through squares as shown.

4. Match marked piece with a 6" x 10" leaf print, right sides facing. Stitch ¼" seam on both sides of diagonal lines. Press. Cut on all drawn lines to get 4 F triangle-squares.

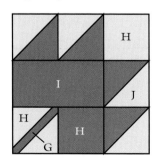

6" Maple Leaf Block—Make 38.

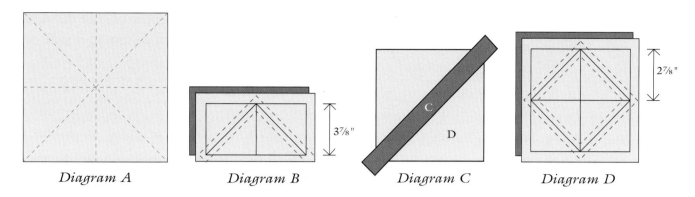

Diagram A   Diagram B   Diagram C   Diagram D

5. Fold each C strip in thirds, wrong sides facing, and press. Center strip on a tan D square *(Diagram C)*; appliqué. Trim strip ends even with square.

6. For each 9" block, select 4 F triangle-squares, 1 C/D unit, 1 E, and 1 D square, all of same print fabric. Sew D to 1 side of C/D unit *(Maple Leaf Block Assembly Diagram)*. Press seam allowance toward D. Sew combined unit to 1 long edge of E. Press seam allowance toward E.

7. Join 2 F triangle-squares as shown. Sew these to top of E. Press seam allowances toward E.

8. Join remaining F triangle-squares and 1 tan D square as shown. Press seam allowances away from center square. Sew combined unit to right side of E to complete block. Make 8 (9") Maple Leaf blocks, using a

different fabric for each block.

9. On wrong side of each tan 7½" square, mark a 2-square by 2-square grid of 2⅞" squares, leaving a 1" margin on all sides *(Diagram D)*. Draw a diagonal line through each square as shown. Match marked piece with a leaf print square, right sides facing. Stitch ¼" seam on

both sides of diagonal lines. Press. Cut on all drawn lines to get 8 J triangle-squares, 4 for each of 2 blocks.

10. Fold each G strip in thirds, wrong sides facing, and press. Center strip on a tan H square and appliqué. Trim ends of strip even with edges of square.

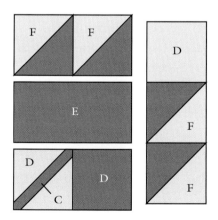

*Maple Leaf Block
Assembly Diagram*

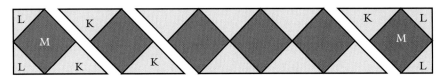

Sashing Assembly Diagram

11. For each 6" block, select 4 J triangle-squares, 1 G/H unit, an I piece, and 1 H square, all of same print fabric. Assemble block as for larger block. Make 38 (6") Maple Leaf blocks.

Quilt Top Assembly

1. For sashing, use 6 M squares, 10 K triangles, and 4 L triangles. Stitch Ks to opposite sides of 4 squares (*Sashing Assembly Diagram*). Press seam allowances toward M. Sew 2 Ls to adjacent sides of each remaining M square as shown; then stitch a K triangle to third side. Join units in a row. Make 16 sashing units.

2. Lay out Oak Leaf blocks in 4 horizontal rows, with 3 blocks in each row (*Row Assembly Diagram*). Lay sashing between blocks and at row ends. When satisfied with placement, join blocks and sashing in each row.

3. For each sashing row, select 42 K triangles, 4 L triangles, and 22 M squares. Join units in a horizontal row in same manner as vertical sashing units. Make 5 sashing rows.

4. Referring to photo, join block rows and sashing rows to complete quilt center.

5. For each side border, select 2 (9") blocks, 10 (6") blocks, 8 Ns, 6 Os, and 6 Ps. Lay out units in a vertical row (*Side Border Diagram*), turning blocks to get a look of wind-tossed leaves (no 2 borders need be alike). When satisfied with placement, sew N strips to opposite sides of 4 (6") blocks and Ps to 1 side of remaining 6" blocks.

6. Join units in each row.

7. From tan fabric reserved for borders, cut 8 (2"-wide) strips. Join pairs end-to-end to make inner border for each quilt side.

Measure length of quilt through center; trim 2 strips to match length (about 88"). Sew a leaf border to each strip, easing to fit as needed. Sew borders to quilt sides. Press seam allowances toward tan borders.

8. For top border, select 2 (9") blocks, 9 (6") blocks, 8 Ns, 6 Os, 5 Ps, and 2 Q pieces. Lay out units in a horizontal row (*Top/Bottom Border Diagram*), turning blocks as desired. Sew Ns and Ps to 6" blocks. Join units in a row. Assemble bottom border in same manner.

9. Measure quilt width through center, including side borders. Trim remaining 2 tan strips to match width (about 88"). Sew leaf border to each strip; then sew borders to top and bottom edges of quilt.

10. Cut remaining tan border fabric into 12 (2"-wide) strips. Join 3 strips end-to-end for each border. Measure length of quilt through center and trim 2 borders to match length. Sew borders to quilt sides. Repeat for top and bottom borders.

Quilting and Finishing

Outline-quilt patchwork and around appliqués. Quilt shown also has crosshatched lines, spaced 2" apart, quilted in Oak Leaf blocks.

Make bias or straight-grain binding. Bind quilt edges.

Block Row—Make 4.

Sashing Row—Make 5.

Row Assembly Diagram

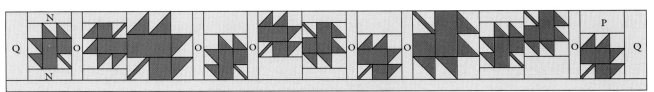

Top/Bottom Border—Make 2.

78

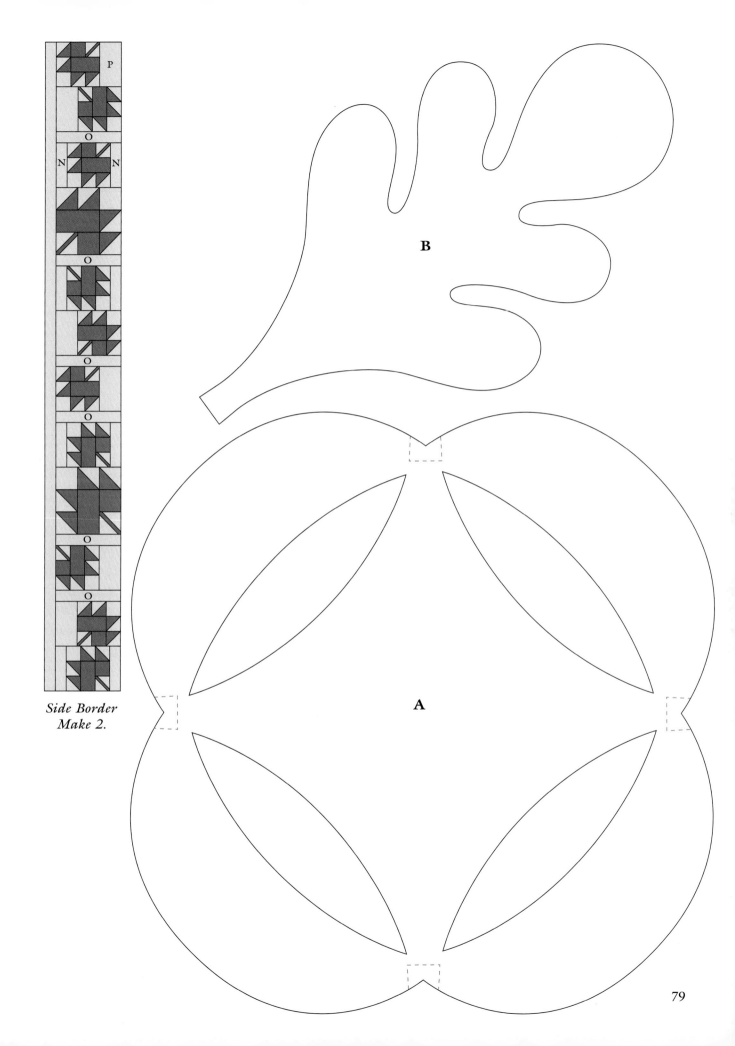

*Side Border
Make 2.*

B

A

P

N

N N

O

O

O

O

O

79

Carol Thomas
Corydon, Iowa

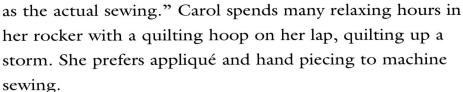

*L*ike many retired people, Carol Thomas needed a way to stay busy and involved when she gave up full-time employment outside the home. So she became a quilter.

"Quilting plays a big part in my life now that my children have their own homes and families," Carol says. "I enjoy drafting patterns and figuring the math as much as the actual sewing." Carol spends many relaxing hours in her rocker with a quilting hoop on her lap, quilting up a storm. She prefers appliqué and hand piecing to machine sewing.

> *"I enjoy drafting patterns and figuring the math as much as the actual sewing."*

Carol started sewing as a child, when her grandmother taught her to hem dishtowels. She got hooked on quilting years ago when she attended a quilt symposium in Ames, home of Iowa State University.

Carol belongs to a church group that quilts one afternoon a week. "My quilt friends are a wonderful mix of people," she says. "I'm especially glad to see younger generations getting so involved."

Carol is a member of the Laplander's Quilt Guild of Wayne County.

Sweet Dreams
1996

Sometimes you come up with that perfect combination of everything you love in one magical quilt. For Carol Thomas, *Sweet Dreams* is that outstanding quilt.

Carol started this quilt with the appliqué, one of her favorite quilting techniques. Carol is an accomplished appliquéist, who enjoys using patterns as well as creating her own designs.

The colors for the appliqué and piecing "just fell into place from my fabric stash," Carol says. Since lavender with rose is a favorite color combination, she had a lot of those fabrics on hand, adding soft greens, blue, and little smattering of yellow.

For the piecing, Carol chose her favorite block, Sister's Choice (also sometimes known as Father's Choice).

Sweet Dreams was judged Best of Show at the 1998 Laplander's Guild show and was seen at the 1998 American Quilter's Society show in Paducah, Kentucky.

Sweet Dreams

Finished Size
Quilt: 92½" x 111"
Blocks: 144 (6¼" x 6¼")

Materials
34 (9½" x 17") dark pastel prints and solids for piecing
15 (8" x 15") medium pastel prints and solids for piecing
18 (8" x 15") light pastel prints and solids for piecing
Scraps or ⅛ yard *each* of the following for appliqué:
   8 pink prints, 4 yellow prints, 4 lilac prints, 1 medium blue print, 1 light blue print, and 3 green solids (light, medium, and bright medium)
1 yard dark green
4¾ yards muslin
4¾ yards lilac (includes binding)*
3¼ yards 108"-wide backing
¼"-wide bias pressing bar (optional)
*Note: Lilac yardage is for cross-grain border strips. For lengthwise border strips, you'll need 5½ yards. But be warned—borders are very long and will be difficult to cut lengthwise.

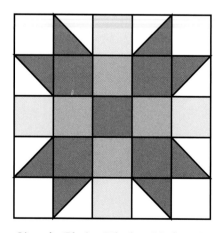

Sister's Choice Block—Make 144.

Pieces to Cut
Instructions are for rotary cutting and quick piecing. Cut all strips cross-grain except as noted. Cut pieces in order listed to get best use of yardage. Set appliqué fabrics aside until needed.

From muslin
• 2 (8"-wide) cross-grain strips and 2 (10" x 58") lengthwise strips for center borders.
• 1 (10½" x 58") lengthwise strip for pillow tuck.
• 9 (9½"-wide) strips. From these, cut 36 (9½") squares for block triangle-squares.
• 25 (1¾"-wide) strips. From these and scrap, cut 576 (1¾") squares for blocks.

From lilac
• Set aside 3 yards for borders (3⅝ yards for lengthwise borders) and 1 yard for binding.
• Add ¼ yard to fabrics for appliqué.
• 2 (9½" x 17") pieces; add these to dark piecing fabrics.
• 3 (8" x 15") pieces; add these to medium piecing fabrics.

From each dark pastel print (including lilac)
• 1 (9½") square for triangle-squares for blocks.
• 4 (1¾" x 9½") strips. From these, cut 20 (1¾") squares for blocks.

From each medium (including lilac) and each light pastel fabric
• 4 (1¾" x 15") strips. From these, cut 32 (1¾") squares for blocks.

Block Assembly
1. On wrong side of each 9½" muslin square, draw a 4-square by 4-square grid of 2⅛" squares, leaving a 1" margin on all sides

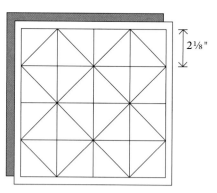

Diagram A

(Diagram A). Draw diagonal lines through squares as shown.
2. Match each marked muslin square with a 9½" dark pastel square, right sides facing. Stitch a ¼" seam on both sides of each diagonal line. Press.
3. Cut on all drawn lines to get 32 triangle-squares from each grid. Press seam allowances toward dark fabric.
4. For 1 block, select 8 triangle-squares, 5 squares of same dark pastel fabric, 4 medium pastel squares, 4 light pastel squares, and 4 muslin squares.
5. Join dark and medium squares in 3 rows *(Diagram B)*. Press seam allowances toward dark fabric. Join rows to complete center nine-patch.

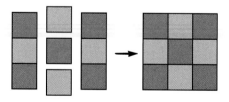

Diagram B

6. Sew 2 triangle-squares to opposite sides of each light square *(Block Assembly Diagram)*. Press seam allowances toward light square. Join 2 of these units to sides of nine-patch as shown. Press seam allowances toward nine-patch.

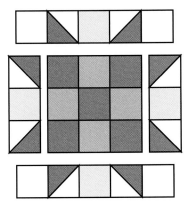

Block Assembly Diagram

7. Sew muslin squares to ends of 2 remaining units. Press seam allowances toward muslin. Join rows to top and bottom edges of nine-patch to complete block. Make 144 blocks.

8. Select 36 blocks for center medallion. Referring to photo, lay out blocks in 6 rows with 6 blocks in each row. When satisfied with placement, join blocks in each row. Then join rows.

9. From lilac border fabric, cut 4 (3"-wide) cross-grain strips. Sew strips to sides of medallion and miter corners.

Appliqué

1. Measure length through middle of pieced medallion. Trim 8"-wide muslin border strips to match length. Sew borders to medallion sides, easing to fit as needed. Press seam allowances toward borders.

2. Measure width of medallion through middle; trim 10"-wide muslin strips to match width. Sew these to top and bottom edges of medallion.

3. From dark green, cut a 24" square. Cut square in half diagonally. Starting at cut edge of each triangle, cut ¾"-wide bias strips. (Vine segments are short, so it's

not necessary to make continuous bias.) Press each strip in thirds to ¼"-wide (use pressing bar, if desired).

4. From assorted fabrics, cut pieces for 14 pink roses and 10 lilac roses (patterns C–G). Pin a pink rose at corners of muslin border and at center of top and bottom borders. Pin a lilac rose at center of each side border.

5. Referring to *Appliqué Placement Diagram,* cut pieces for remaining flowers and leaves in colors of your choice. Pin flowers on each border, adding lengths of vine as needed. (On quilt shown, vine lengths vary from 1" to 6½".) Referring to photo, place remaining pink and lilac roses as shown.

6. When satisfied with placement, appliqué pieces in place.

7. For pillow tuck, cut pieces for 3 lilac roses and 4 pink roses. Referring to photo, pin a lilac rose at center and a pink rose at each corner of 10½" muslin strip. Cut pieces for remaining flowers and leaves. Pin flowers in place, adding lengths of vine as needed. Place remaining pink and lilac roses as shown. When satisfied with placement, appliqué pieces in place.

Quilt Top Assembly

1. From remaining lilac fabric, cut 25 (3"-wide) cross-grain strips. From these, piece 4 (70"-long) borders. Sew borders to medallion edges and miter corners.

2. Select 30 blocks. Join these into 3 horizontal rows, with 10 blocks in each row. Referring to photo, sew 2 rows to bottom

Appliqué Placement Diagram

edge of medallion. Sew remaining row to top edge. Press seam allowances toward medallion.

3. Cut 2 (17"-long) borders and piece 2 (70"-long) borders for pillow tuck. Stitch borders to muslin strip and miter corners. Stitch pillow tuck unit to top row of blocks.

4. Join 10 blocks in a row. Sew row to top edge of pillow tuck.

5. Join remaining blocks in 4 vertical rows, with 17 blocks in each row. Referring to photo, sew 2 rows to each side of quilt.

6. Piece 2 (96"-long) borders and 2 (115"-long) borders. Sew borders to quilt; miter corners.

Quilting and Finishing

Outline-quilt piecing and appliqué. Background spaces around appliqué are quilted with cross-hatched lines spaced ¾" apart.

Quilt shown has flowers quilted in each lilac border (see quilting pattern on facing page; for tips on making a quilting stencil, see page 99). Mark flowers on border corners; then space flowers evenly on each border, adjusting length of connecting lines as needed.

Make bias or straight-grain binding from reserved lilac fabric. Bind quilt edges.

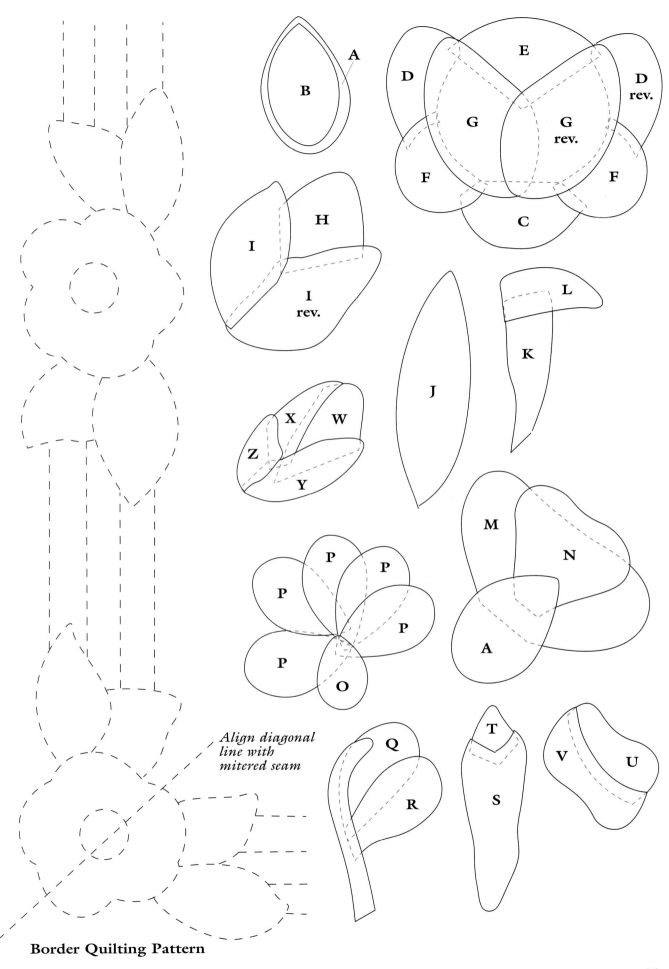

Border Quilting Pattern

Align diagonal line with mitered seam

85

Joan K. Streck
Overland Park, Kansas

A life-long passion for quilting is Joan Streck's legacy from her grandmother.

Joan's grandmother left two quilts unfinished when she died. Despite her sewing skills, Joan had no quiltmaking experience. There were few quilting books available in 1969, but Joan looked at old quilts for guidance and gave it a try.

Though her quilting stitches were not very good when she started, they got better. By the time the first quilt was done, "I loved it—I was hooked!" Joan says.

Joan goes to quilt shows and conventions, taking classes whenever she can. "I always come away from a workshop with at least one new idea or a hint on how to make quilting faster and better," she says.

> *"I always come away from a workshop with at least one new idea."*

Joan enjoys traveling with her husband to visit their children and grandchildren—there are always interesting quilt shops to explore along the way.

Joan is a member of the Quilters Guild of Greater Kansas City, the Kansas Quilters Organization, and the Blue Valley Quilters Guild, as well as national quilters' groups. Her quilt-show ribbons include one from the 1995 American Quilter's Society show in Paducah, Kentucky.

Dizzy Geese
1997

Shelly Burge of Lincoln, Nebraska, teaches a workshop on the design and use of the traditional Flying Geese motif to fit any space. It must be a wonderful class, because look what Joan Streck got out of it—the idea for *Dizzy Geese*.

"I had an old pattern called Tiled Wedding Ring that I wanted to use in a new way," Joan recalls. She redrew the design with a star inside a ring of flying geese, and then squared off the block with a corner triangle.

Dizzy Geese is Joan's first attempt at designing a quilt "from scratch." In addition to designing the block, she added pieced sashing to create small stars within the galaxy of blocks. The quilt is pieced and quilted by hand.

Show-goers saw *Dizzy Geese* at the 1997 Blue Valley Quilters Guild show and at the 1998 national quilt show at Silver Dollar City, Branson, Missouri, where it won a third place and judge's choice ribbons.

Dizzy Geese

Finished Size
Quilt: 74½" x 93"
Blocks: 12 (17" x 17")

Materials
8½ yards cream tone-on-tone print (includes binding)
15 fat quarters or scraps (mostly solids, plaids, and stripes)
⅛ yard tan print
5⅝ yards backing fabric

Pieces to Cut
Cut all strips cross-grain except as noted.

From cream
- Set aside 2½ yards for borders and binding.
- 13 (2¾"-wide) strips. From these, cut 48 (2¾") B squares and 104 of Pattern H.
- 3 (4"-wide) strips. From these, cut 48 of Pattern D.
- 42 (2"-wide) strips. From these, cut 576 (2") E squares and 176 (2" x 3½") F pieces.
- 3 (4⅛"-wide) strips. From these, cut 26 (4⅛") squares. Cut each square in half diagonally to get 52 G triangles.
- 8 (6"-wide) strips. From these, cut 26 (6") squares. Cut each

square in half diagonally to get 52 I triangles.
- 1 (17½" x 42") piece. From this, cut 17 (2" x 17½") sashing strips.
- 24 (1¼") K squares.

From scraps
- 12 (5") A squares.
- 12 same-fabric sets of 4 of Pattern C and 4 of Pattern C reversed (1 set for each block).
- 48 (2" x 21") strips. From these, cut 288 (2" x 3½") F rectangles.
- 32 (2"-wide) strips. From these, cut 352 (2") E squares.

From tan print
- 6 (2") J squares.
- 48 (1¼") K squares.

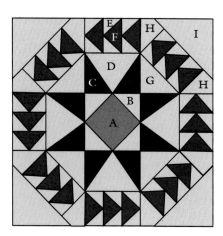

Dizzy Geese Block—Make 12.

Quilt Top Assembly
1. For 1 block, select 1 A, 4 B squares, 1 set of C/C rev. triangles, and 4 Ds.
2. See Quilt Smart instructions on page 91 for tips on diagonal-corner technique. Sew B squares to 4 corners of A square. Press seam allowances toward A.
3. Sew C and C rev. triangles to sides of each D (*Block Diagram*). Press seam allowances toward D. Make 4 C/D units.
4. Select 24 scrap F rectangles and 48 cream E squares. Use diagonal-corner technique to sew an E to 2 corners of each F (*Diagram A*). Press seam allowances toward Es. Join 3 geese in

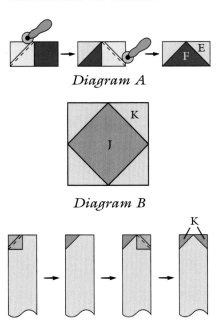

Block Assembly Diagram

Row 1

Sashing Row

Row 2

Row Assembly Diagram

a row. Make 8 geese rows.

5. Select 4 rows for corners. Sew H pieces to both ends of each row *(Block Assembly Diagram)*. Press seam allowances toward H. Then sew G and I triangles to opposite sides of unit as shown. Press seam allowances toward G and I. Make 4 corner units.

6. Sew remaining 4 geese rows to D edge of C/D units. Press seam allowances toward D.

7. Lay out units in 3 horizontal rows as shown *(Block Assembly Diagram)*. Join units in rows; then join rows to complete block. Make 12 blocks.

Diagram A

Diagram B

Diagram C

8. Using diagonal-corner technique, sew cream K squares to 4 corners of each J square *(Diagram B)*. In same manner, sew tan K squares to 1 end of each sashing strip *(Diagram C)*. Set aside 10 strips; then sew remaining tan squares to opposite end of remaining 7 sashing strips.

9. Lay out 2 rows of 3 blocks each, inserting sashing between blocks *(Row Assembly Diagram)*. For Row 1, use sashing with 1 sewn end. For Row 2, use sashing with 2 sewn ends. Between block rows, lay out a Sashing Row as shown. When satisfied with placement, join units in each row. Repeat to make bottom half of quilt.

10. Referring to photo, lay out rows to verify placement. Join rows to complete quilt center.

Borders

1. Use scrap E squares and cream Fs to make 176 geese units for borders.

2. From fabric reserved for borders, cut 4 (3¾"-wide) lengths for inner border and 4 (4½"-wide) lengths for outer border. Save remainder for binding.

3. Measure quilt length through middle of pieced top. Trim 2 inner border strips to match length. Measure width of pieced top through middle; trim remaining inner border strips to match width.

4. For each side border, sew 46 geese end-to-end. Match length of geese row with precut side border. You have enough geese units to add 1 more if needed to match border length. Sew geese rows to side borders, referring to photo for correct position of each row. (Note that on left border, geese fly south; on right border, they fly north.) Ease geese to fit borders as needed. Then sew joined borders to quilt sides, easing to fit quilt top. Press all seam allowances toward cream border.

5. Join 34 geese end-to-end for top border. Match length to precut top border, adding 1 more geese unit if needed. Sew geese to top border with geese flying west. Repeat for bottom border, positioning geese flying east.

6. Join 3 geese units with G, H, and I pieces to make each corner unit as before. Referring to photo, sew corners to ends of top and bottom borders.

7. Sew borders to top and bottom edges of quilt top.

8. Measure length of quilt top through middle as before. Trim 2 outer border strips to match length. Sew these to quilt sides, easing to fit as needed. Repeat for top and bottom borders. Press seam allowances toward outer borders.

Quilting and Finishing

Outline-quilt patchwork. Quilt shown also has a cable quilted in each cream border.

Make straight-grain binding from remaining cream fabric.

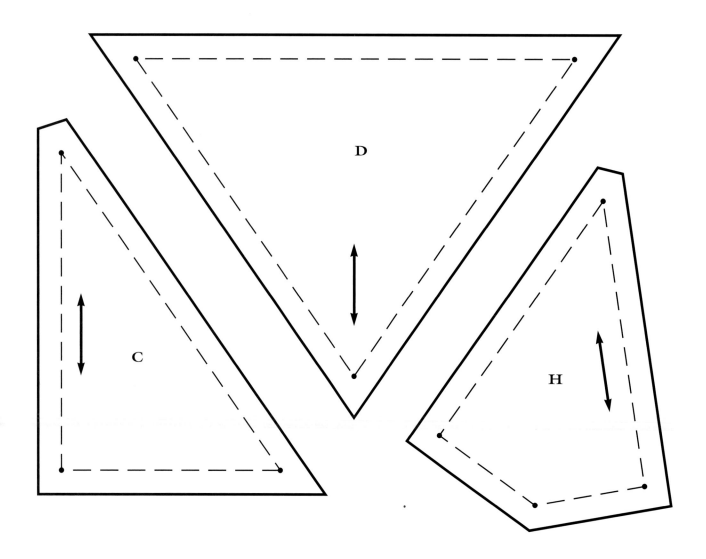

place, aligning stems with placement guides and tucking stem ends under A. Pin a D at top of each E. Pin C and C reversed leaves at sides of each E stem.

3. When satisfied with placement of pieces, appliqué Ds and Es in place. Then stitch all C leaves. Appliqué A, covering bottom edges of Cs and Es. Sew B in place in A center.

4. See Quilt Smart tips on page 99 to make a stencil of quilting design (see pattern, page 99). Aligning stencil with placement guides, lightly mark complete quilting design on each of 6 setting squares. Mark ½ design on setting triangles and ¼ design on corner triangles in same manner, folding each triangle in half to create a placement guide.

5. Lay out blocks in 6 diagonal rows as shown, alternating appliquéd blocks and setting squares *(Quilt Assembly Diagram)*. End rows with setting triangles as shown. When satisfied with placement, join blocks in rows.

6. Join rows to complete quilt center. Sew corner triangles in place as shown.

Borders

1. Join 2"-wide green strips end-to-end to get 4 (88"-long) inner border strips.

2. Join 1½"-wide green strips end-to-end in same manner to get 2 (110"-long) strips for side borders and 2 (88"-long) strips for top and bottom borders.

3. Mark centers of each green and cream border strip. Matching centers, sew 2"-wide and 1½"-wide green borders to

Quilt Assembly Diagram

opposite sides of each cream border strip. Press seam allowances toward green.

4. Sew borders to quilt, mitering corners.

5. Referring to photo, pin F pieces in place, aligning F center with mitered seam. Pin A and B pieces at F ends as shown.

6. Center 1 G on top border. Pin A/B pieces at ends of G to complete swag unit. Highest and lowest points of unit should be approximately 1¼" from green border seams.

7. Pin swag units between corners and center unit as shown.

When satisfied with placement, appliqué pieces in place.

8. Repeat steps 6 and 7 for bottom border.

9. Space 4 swag units evenly along length of each side border. When satisfied with placement, appliqué pieces in place.

Quilting and Finishing

Outline-quilt around appliqués. Then work marked quilting in setting squares and triangles. Fill border background with vertical lines spaced 1" apart.

Make bias or straight-grain binding. Bind quilt edges.

95

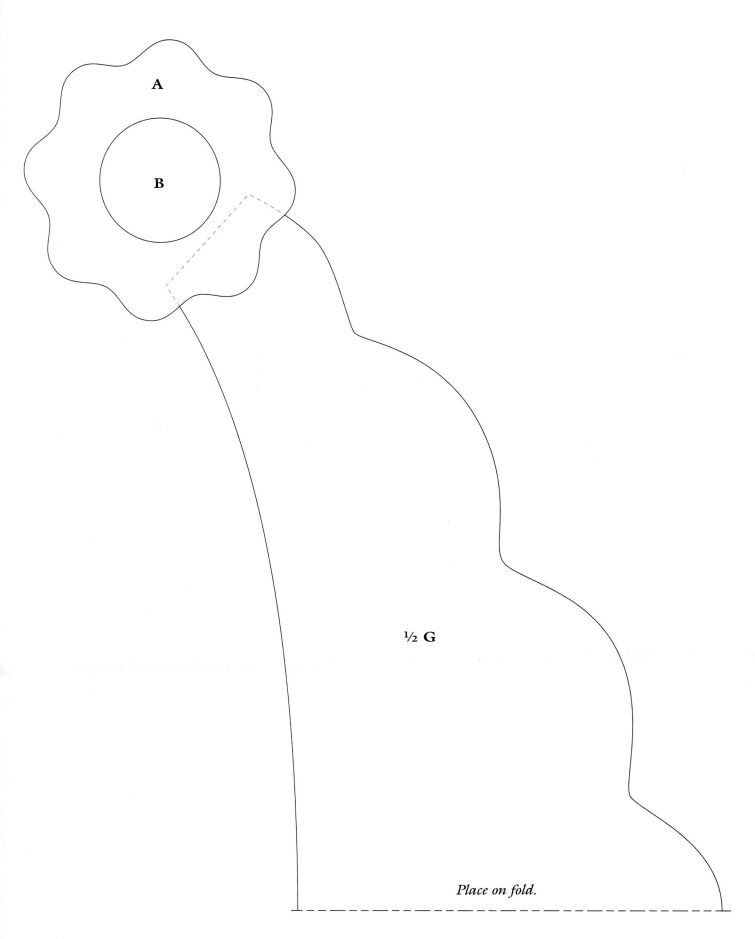

A

B

½ G

Place on fold.

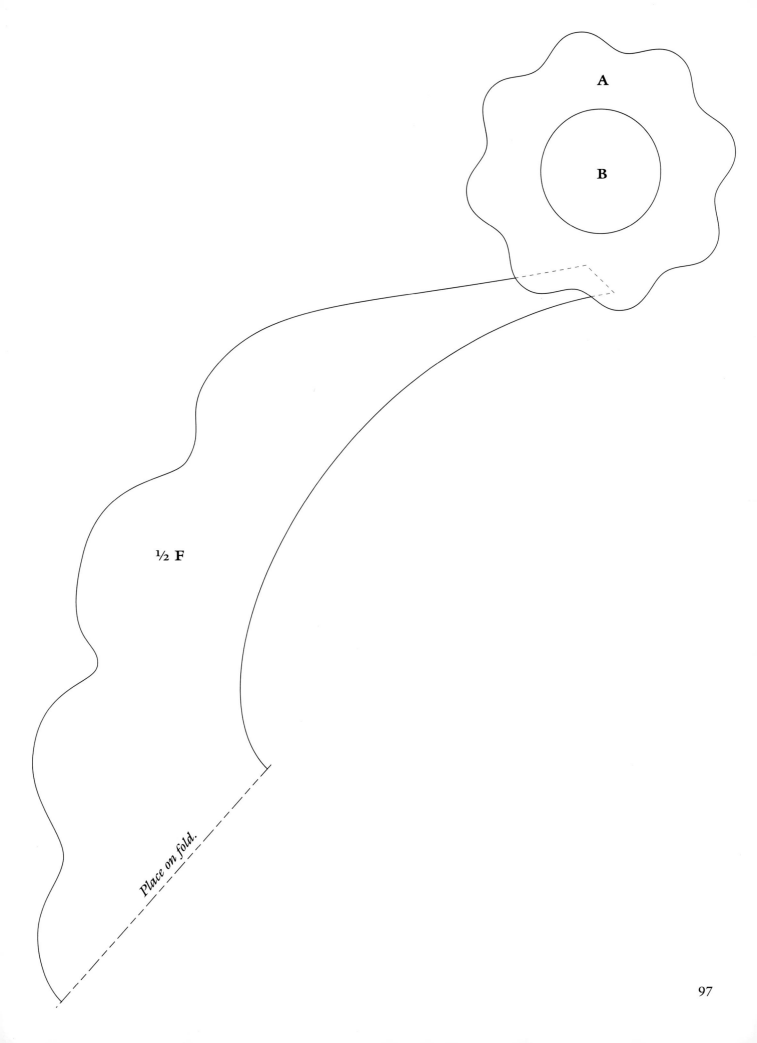

A

B

½ F

Place on fold.

97

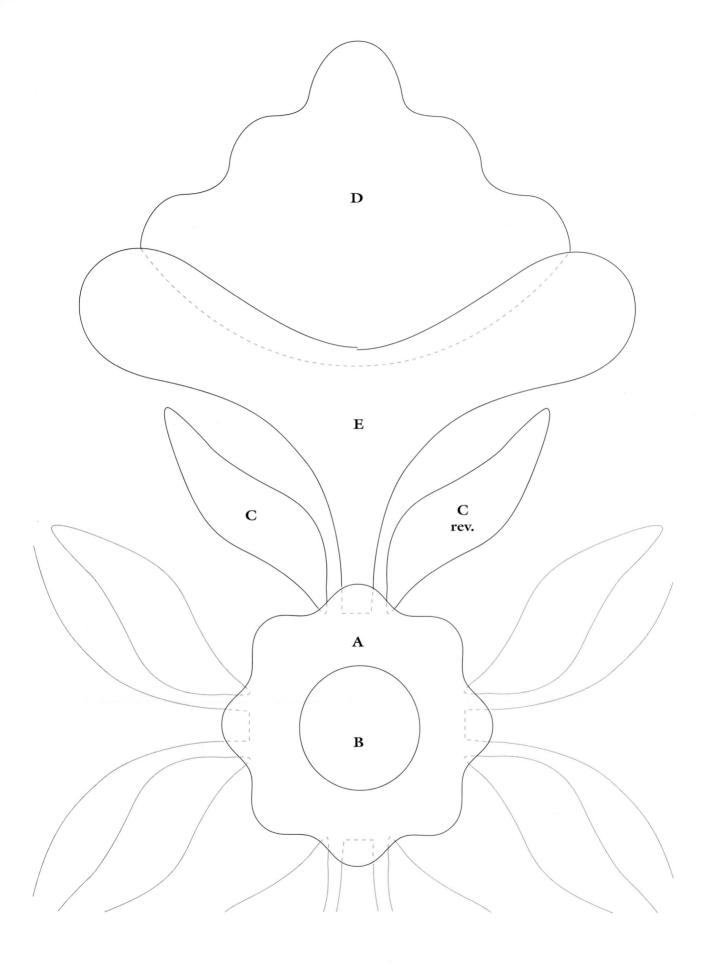

D

E

C

C
rev.

A

B

❖QUILT SMART❖

Making a Stencil of a Quilting Design

1. Trace quilting design onto freezer paper. Include placement lines, if any.

2. Use a craft knife to cut little slots or dots along traced lines of the design.

3. Place stencil on right side of fabric, aligning stencil's placement lines with creased guidelines on fabric.

4. Select a fine-tipped chalk or lead pencil for marking. Always test the marker on a fabric scrap to be sure it washes out.

5. Make a light but visible mark on the fabric through each slot in the stencil until design is complete (*photo,* below). Heavy marks are hard to wash out.

6. Use a ruler or yardstick to mark straight lines of quilting.

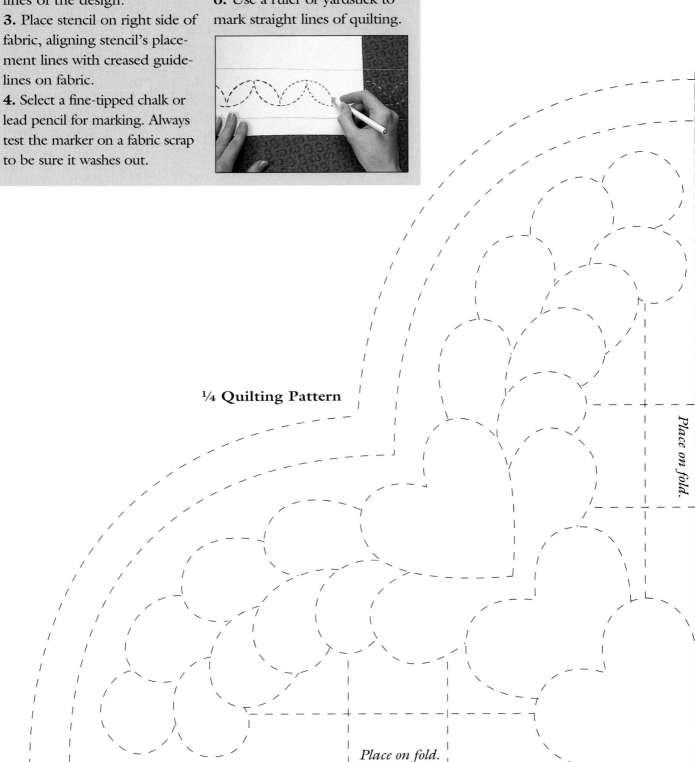

¼ Quilting Pattern

Place on fold.

Place on fold.

Carolyn Roller Miller
McKinney, Texas

When Carolyn Miller's husband retired, she decided to find a hobby. "I needed something to do so we wouldn't drive each other crazy," says Carolyn. Little did she know what she was starting when she bought her first quilt book and a Bernina sewing machine in 1992.

She had admired quilts for a few years before she set out to make one herself. Carolyn was an experienced sewer, "so all I had to do was adjust the seam allowance from ⅝" to ¼"," she says. "And a quilt is easier because it doesn't have to fit a body."

"It is so important for us to label our quilts for future owners."

The more she learned about quilts, the more Carolyn realized she was inspired by antique quilts. She collects nineteenth-century quilts, examining them closely and using the designs and quilting patterns in her own work. Whenever possible, Carolyn researches a quilt's personal history. This has taught her why "it is so important for us to label our quilts for future owners." (See Quilt Smart on page 72.)

While Carolyn's husband works in his home office, she stays out of his way with four or five quilts in progress. She says, "Making quilts, collecting and studying them means never being bored."

Carolyn is a member of the McKinney Quilt Guild and the Allen Quilt Guild, as well as national quilters' groups. *Tie a Yellow Ribbon* was Best of Show at the 1998 Azalea Quilt Show and a judge's choice at the 1998 Dallas Quilt Show. It also earned awards at the 1998 National Quilter's Society show and the International Quilter's Society show in Houston.

Tie a Yellow Ribbon
1998

Carolyn Miller makes quilts that reflect her love of antique quilts. *Tie a Yellow Ribbon* was inspired by a classic Carpenter's Square design.

For the border design, Carolyn looked at pictures of hundreds of quilts until she found the right one to adapt. She completed the piecing and the appliqué on her Bernina sewing machine.

Carolyn designed lovely feather quilting motifs for the open areas of the quilt. Highlighted by beautifully stitched stippling, the feathers are machine-quilted and trapuntoed. Patterns for these quilting designs are on pages 104, 106, and 107.

101

Tie a Yellow Ribbon

Finished Size
Quilt: 83½" x 83½"
Blocks: 13 (15" x 15")

Materials
6 yards cream print or muslin
4 yards navy print
2 yards yellow/gold print
2½ yards 90"-wide backing

Pieces to Cut
Instructions are for rotary cutting quick piecing, and traditional appliqué. Appliqué patterns are on pages 105 and 106.

Cut strips cross-grain except as noted. Cut pieces in order listed for most efficient use of yardage.

From navy
- 1 (32") square for binding.
- 43 (1½"-wide) strips for units A, B, and D.
- 7 (4"-wide) strips. From these, cut 28 of Pattern Y.

From cream
- Set aside 2½ yards for borders.
- 36 (1½"-wide) strips for units A, B, and D.

- 6 (5½"-wide) strips. From these, cut 4 (5½" x 15½") E pieces, 8 (5½" x 11") F pieces, and 17 (5½") C squares.
- 1 (10"-wide) strip. From this, cut 4 (10") squares. Cut each square in half diagonally to get 8 G triangles.
- 2 (13") squares. Cut each square in half diagonally to get 4 corner triangles.

From yellow/gold print
- 7 (4½"-wide) strips. From these, cut 28 of Pattern X.
- 3 (5"-wide) strips. From these, cut 24 bows and 4 corner bows.
- 3 (3"-wide) strips. From these, cut 56 tassels.
- 7 (1½"-wide) strips. Set aside for tassel ribbons.
- 8 (⅞"-wide) strips for binding flange (optional).

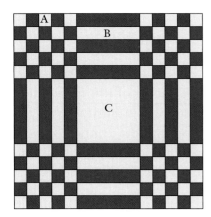

Block 1—Make 9.

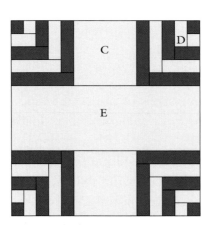

Block 2—Make 4.

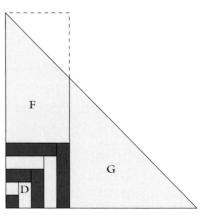

Side Unit—Make 8.

Quilt Top Assembly

1. Use 1½"-wide strips to make strip sets *(Strip Set Diagrams)*. Make 8 of Strip Set 1, joining 3 navy strips and 2 cream strips in each set. Make 4 of Strip Set 2, joining 3 cream strips and 2 navy strips. Press seam allowances toward navy in all strip sets.

2. From Strip Set 1, cut 36 (5½"-wide) segments for Unit B. Then cut 72 (1½"-wide) segments for Unit A.

3. From Strip Set 2, cut 108 (1½"-wide) A segments.

4. Select 2 segments from Strip Set 1 and 3 segments from Strip Set 2 for each Unit A. Join segments to complete unit *(Unit A Assembly Diagram)*.

5. Select 4 of Unit A, 4 of Unit B, and 1 C square for each Block 1. Referring to block diagram, join units in rows. Press seam allowances toward B units. Then join rows to complete block. Make 9 of Block 1.

6. Use remaining 1½"-wide strips for Unit D. Cut 1½" squares of each color and join *(Unit D Assembly Diagram)*. Add a cream strip to bottom edge and trim even with

squares. Continue adding navy and cream strips log-cabin style, until unit is complete as shown. Make 24 of Unit D.

7. Select 4 of Unit D, 1 Unit E, and 2 C squares for each Block 2. Referring to block diagram, join C and D units in rows. Press seam allowances toward

Cs. Then join rows to complete block. Make 4 of Block 2.

8. Select 1 Unit D, 1 F, and 1 G for each Side Unit. Sew F to 1 side of D. Press seam allowance toward D. Then sew G to D/F, aligning bottom of triangle with edge of D as shown in unit diagram. Align a ruler with edge of G and rotary-cut excess fabric from F. Make 8 units.

9. Lay out blocks in 5 rows, alternating Block 1 and Block 2 in each row *(Quilt Assembly Diagram)*. Except for center row, add Side Units to row ends as shown. When satisfied with placement, join units in each row.

10. Lay out rows to verify placement. Join rows. Then add corner triangles as shown.

Quilt Assembly Diagram

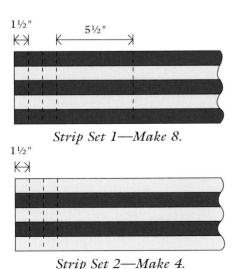

1½"

5½"

Strip Set 1—Make 8.

1½"

Strip Set 2—Make 4.

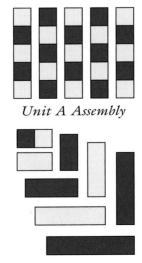

Unit A Assembly

Unit D Assembly

Borders

1. From fabric reserved for borders, cut 4 (10½" x 90") strips for border. Sew borders to quilt sides and miter corners. (*Note:* Carolyn didn't miter corners on her quilt, but we thought a mitered seam would help with appliqué placement.)

2. Prepare bow and scallop pieces for appliqué.

3. To make tassel ribbons, fold each 1½"-wide gold strip in half lengthwise, wrong sides facing. Stitch ¼" from raw edges to make a narrow tube. Press seam allowances open, centered on 1 side of pressed strip.

4. For each corner bow, cut 2 (5"-long) ribbons. Referring to photo on page 102, pin corner bow, ribbons, and 2 tassels in place on mitered seam.

5. Cut 48 (4½"-long) ribbon pieces for remaining bows.

6. Working out from corners, pin 7 scallops on each border, spacing them evenly and layering navy Y pieces over yellow X pieces. Referring to photo, pin bows, ribbons, and tassels between scallops.

7. When satisfied with placement, stitch appliqué pieces in place on each border.

Quilting and Finishing

1. Mark quilting designs on quilt top. Carolyn Miller quilted straight lines over piecing that form an X in each square of Unit A and outline-quilted units B and D. Patterns for feather designs in C units, Block 2, and Side Units are below and on pages 106 and 107. Carolyn outline-quilted appliqué pieces, adding echo quilting below scallops and clamshell quilting above. Quilt as desired.

2. Carolyn added a narrow gold flange between quilt top and binding. Join ⅞"-wide gold strips end-to-end to make a continuous strip 9½ yards long. Press strip in half lengthwise, wrong sides facing. Baste flange to quilt top, matching raw edges and mitering corners.

3. Make bias or straight-grain binding from reserved navy fabric. Bind quilt edges.

Block 1 Quilting Pattern

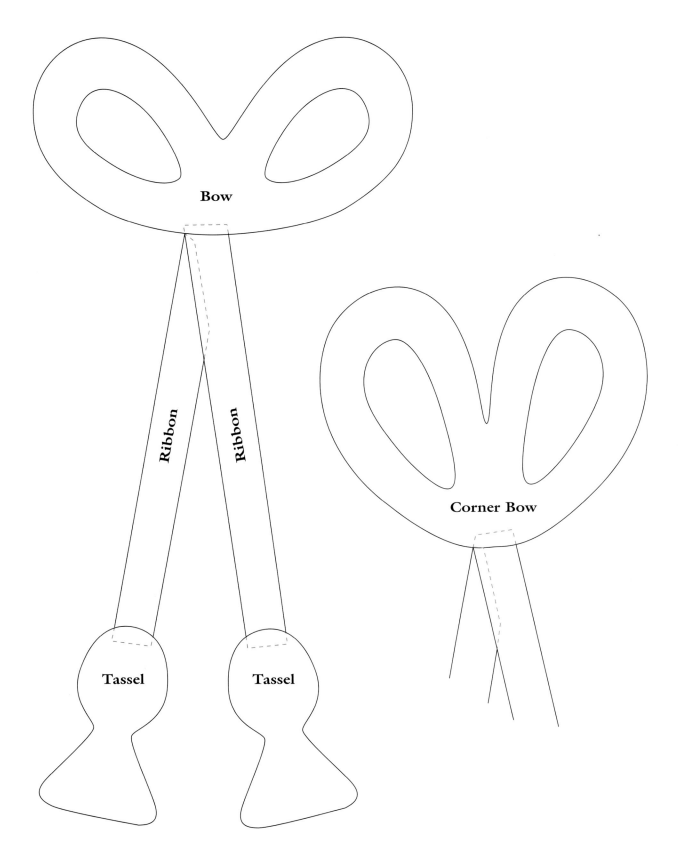

Bow

Ribbon Ribbon

Tassel Tassel

Corner Bow

105

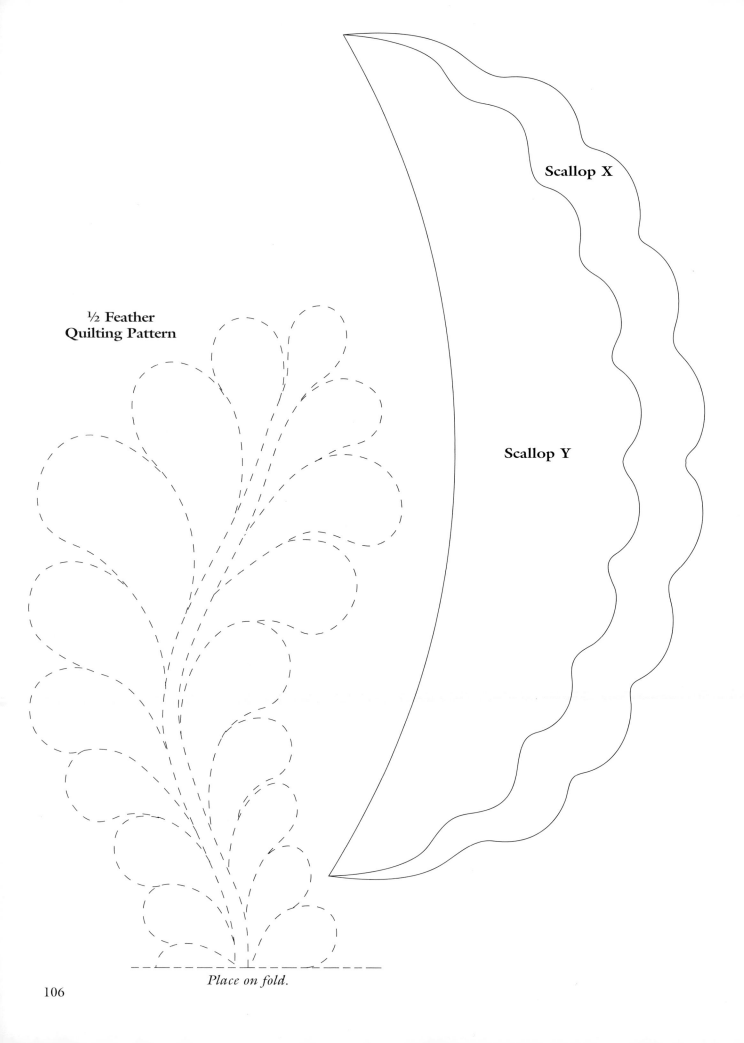

Scallop X

Scallop Y

½ **Feather**
Quilting Pattern

Place on fold.

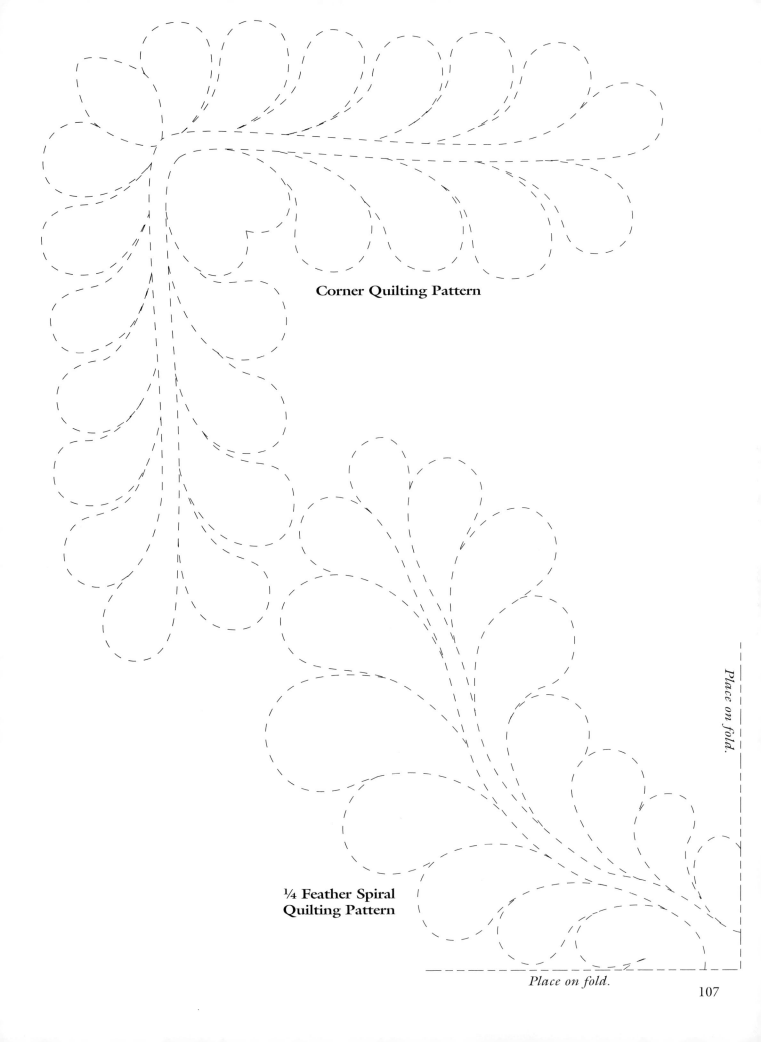

Corner Quilting Pattern

¼ **Feather Spiral
Quilting Pattern**

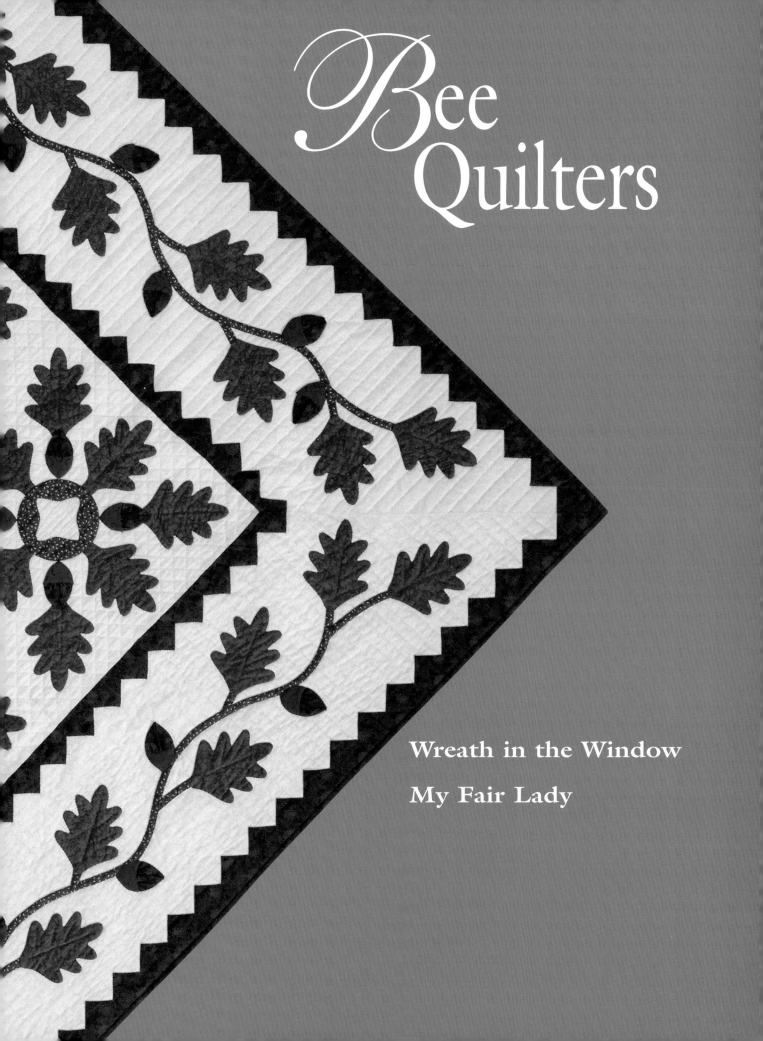

Bee
Quilters

Wreath in the Window

My Fair Lady

Pieceful Scrappers
Toronto, Canada

Back row, left to right: Rhonda Penney, Margaret Sneyd, Edyth Yeomans, Lois Léger. Front row, left to right: Mary Lou Watson, Barbara Pollock, Marion Pilkington.

Whatever the quilt in-progress, the Pieceful Scrappers make it with scraps and by hand.

"Some days, we think quilting *is* our life," says member Mary Lou Watson. Experienced quilters, the seven women of the team are all members of the York Heritage Quilters Guild of Toronto. But with the guild's roster approaching 500, Mary Lou says a "small group gives us up-close and personal stitching time, sharing something we love."

The Scrappers began meeting weekly in 1986. They spend many a productive hour quilting (and chatting) around a large frame, putting more and more quilting into each quilt as time goes by.

"Group quilts are great fun, and a real plus for busy people," says Mary Lou. Even a big quilt like *Wreath in the Window* required each member to make just eight blocks. It was member Barbara Pollock's turn to keep this quilt.

Wreath in the Window
1995

For a group like the Pieceful Scrappers, the challenge of a traditional block is to make it interesting to stitch as well as appropriate for scraps. Selecting the block is the first piece of the puzzle.

For *Wreath in the Window,* the Scrappers gave a star block a completely new look. By using one fabric for the triangles around the center octagon, the star becomes a wreath. For more interest, they created the effect of Attic Windows by using two cream tone-on-tone prints, one slightly darker than the other, for the outer pieces of the block.

The scrap fabrics coordinate with the border fabric, a floral print that "we chose thinking that corner miters would be easy," according to Mary Lou Watson. "We were wrong, but we did it!"

Wreath in the Window was shown at the American Quilter's Society show at Paducah, Kentucky, in 1996. In 1997, the quilt won first prize ribbons at the Waterloo County Quilt Festival and the International Plowing Match. It was Best of Show at the 1997 Markham Fair.

Wreath in the Window

Finished Size

Quilt: 98½" x 108½"*

Blocks: 56 (12" x 12")

*Note: This is a king-size quilt. For a 86½" x 98½" queen-size, make 42 blocks, set 6 across and 7 down.

Materials

3⅜ yards muslin

3¼ yards border fabric (includes binding)

2 yards *each* of 2 beige/tan tone-on-tone prints

½ yard inner border fabric

166 (5" x 9") scraps

8¾ yards backing fabric

Pieces to Cut

Cut all strips crossgrain except as noted.

From muslin

• 56 (6½") A squares.

• 28 (1¾") strips. From these, cut 448 of Pattern C.

From each beige/tan print

• 224 of Pattern E.

From inner border fabric

• 12 (1¼"-wide) strips. Add remaining fabric to scraps.

From scraps

• Set aside 56 scraps for block's inner circle (wreath). From remainder, cut 896 (2⅛") squares. Cut each square in half diagonally to get 1,792 D triangles.

Quilt Top Assembly

1. For each block, select 1 A, 8 Cs, 4 Es of each beige/tan fabric, 32 Ds, and 1 (5" x 9") scrap.

2. From scrap, cut a 3¾" square. Cut this in quarters diagonally to get 4 B triangles. From remainder, cut 4 (2¼") B squares.

3. See Quilt Smart instructions (page 91) for tips on diagonal-corner technique. Sew B squares to 4 corners of A square (*Diagram A*). Press seam allowances toward A.

4. Sew C diamonds to sides of each B triangle (*Diagram B*). Press seam allowances toward Cs. Make 4 B/C units.

5. Select 4 D triangles. Join 2 triangles to make a square; then add 2 more triangles to adjacent sides of square as shown (*Diagram C*). Make 8 D units.

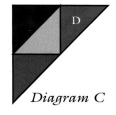

Diagram A

Diagram B

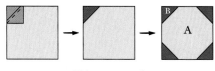

Diagram C

6. Sew a D unit to top of each B/C unit (*Block Assembly Diagram*). Sew 2 joined units to opposite sides of A/B square as

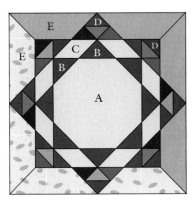

Wreath in the Window Block—Make 56.

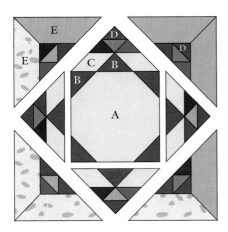

Block Assembly Diagram

shown. Press; then sew 2 units to remaining sides of A/B.

7. To make corner units, sew 2 Es to adjacent sides of each remaining D unit, mitering corners as shown *(Corner Unit Diagram)*. Select Es carefully, referring to block diagrams for correct placement of both beige/tan fabrics. Press seam allowances toward Es.

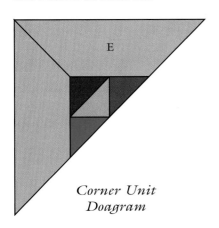

Corner Unit Doagram

8. Sew corner units to block as shown to complete block. Make 56 blocks.

9. Referring to photo, lay out blocks in 8 horizontal rows of 7 blocks each. All blocks are positioned in same manner, not turned, so adjacent E pieces are always contrasting fabrics. Join blocks in rows; then join rows to complete quilt center.

Borders

1. Cut 4 (6"-wide) lengthwise strips from outer border fabric. Set aside remainder for binding.

2. Join inner border strips end-to-end to get 4 (115"-long) strips. Sew an inner border strip to one edge of each outer border, matching center points.

3. Sew borders to quilt, mitering corners.

Quilting and Finishing

Outline-quilt patchwork. Fill center of each block with a grid or floral design. Quilt shown has a lover's knot quilted in X formed by E pieces where blocks meet.

Bind with straight-grain or bias binding made from border fabric.

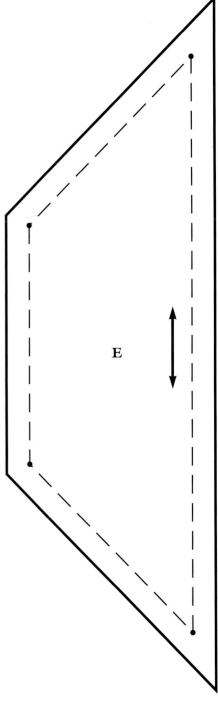

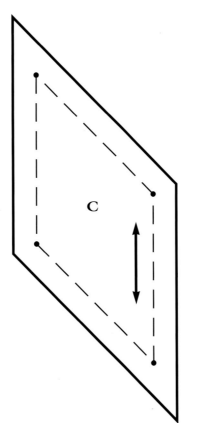

Quilters Guild of Indianapolis, Inc.
Indianapolis, Indiana

*T*he Quilters Guild of Indianapolis is known for its charitable work. "We make comfort quilts for nine organizations in this area," says former guild president Carolyn Shay. "We begin each year's work on the third Saturday of March, National Quilting Day." The guild donated more than 400 quilts in 1998.

Each spring, a meeting is dedicated to presenting quilts to charity representatives. "They tell us wonderful stories about the hearts that our quilts have touched," says Carolyn.

Guild members also enjoy making baby quilts for members with new infants. "Our baby-quilts chairperson is always ready to present a new arrival with its very own quilt at a guild meeting," says Carolyn. "This is a sure way for all of us to get to see each new baby. Great plan, huh?"

My Fair Lady
1997

Play the right tune, and it just might give you inspiration for a quilt. That's what happened in the fall of 1995, as Synthia Howard and Barb Lucas brainstormed ideas for the guild's raffle quilt. Listening to show tunes, Barb and Synthia leafed through books and photos taken at quilt shows.

"Get Me to the Church on Time" and "I Could Have Danced All Night" apparently provided the right energy, because Synthia got an idea from a block she found in Elly Sienkiewicz's book *Design a Baltimore Album Quilt.*

"The Oak Leaf pattern was all the rage at Quilt Market that fall," recalls Synthia. "I decided to add a folded rosebud and ruched flowers."

The work of 80 guild members made the quilt a reality. Money from ticket sales allowed the guild to make a $2,000 donation to the Indianapolis Alzheimer's Association, with enough left over to fund guild programs for the coming year.

Synthia says guild members "felt like winners" when *My Fair Lady* was juried into the American Quilter's Society 1997 show at Paducah, Kentucky.

My Fair Lady

Finished Size

Quilt: 91½" x 107½"
Blocks: 20 (16" x 16")

Materials

10 yards cream or muslin
4¾ yards dark green print
4 yards red print 1 for dogtooth
    border, ruched roses, folded
    rosebuds, and binding
1¾ yards green print for vines
    and center appliqué
1 yard red print 2 for bud bases
8¼ yards backing fabric
⅜"-wide bias pressing bar
Fiberfill (optional)

Pieces to Cut

Cut all strips crossgrain except
as noted.

From cream
•4 (14¼" x 112") lengthwise
    strips for border.
•20 (16½") background
    squares.

From dark green print
•221 oak leaves (A).

From red print 1
•1 yard for binding.
•19 (2½"-wide) strips for dog-
    tooth borders.
•8 (1⅛"-wide) strips for roses.
•10 (3½"-wide) strips. From
    these, cut 120 (3½") squares
    for folded rosebuds.
•4 numbers for date appliqué.

From green print
•30" square. Set aside for bor-
    der vines and stems.
•20 block circles (B).

From red print 2
•120 rosebud bases (C).

Folded Rosebuds

1. Fold 3½" squares in half,
wrong sides facing (*Diagram A*).
2. Fold sides toward center,
overlapping as shown (*Diagram
B*). Baste bottom edges and
gather to fit inside base (C).
3. Stitch base over bottom of
each bud (*Diagram C*).

Quilt Top Assembly

1. Fold background squares in
half crosswise, lengthwise, and
diagonally. Crease folds to make
placement guides for appliqué.
2. For each block, center circle
(B) on placement guides. Pin 8
leaves (A) and 4 buds in place,
aligning them with placement
guides (*Block Diagram*).

Diagram A

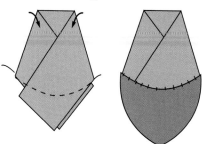

Diagram B   *Diagram C*

3. Appliqué circle and leaves.
Appliqué bud and base as 1
unit. Before completing bud
appliqué, stuff lightly with fiberfill; then complete stitching. If
you prefer, appliqué bud base in

116

Oak Leaf Block—Make 20.

position and leave folded bud free, eliminating filling. Make 20 blocks.

4. Arrange blocks in 5 horizontal rows of 4 blocks each *(Quilt Assembly Diagram)*. Join blocks in rows; then join rows to complete quilt center.

Borders

1. Join 2½"-wide strips of red print 1 to get 2 (68"-long) strips and 2 (84"-long) strips for inner dogtooth border, and 2 (93"-long) strips and 2 (109"-long) strips for outer border. Baste strips onto opposite sides of cream borders, matching raw edges.

2. Join 2 (1⅛"-wide) red print 1 strips end-to-end for each ruched rose. See Quilt Smart instructions on page 118 to

Quilt Assembly Diagram

make 4 roses. Pin a rose in place at center of each border.

3. From 30" green square, make 12½ yards of 1"-wide continuous bias. (See page 144 for tips on making continuous bias.) Fold bias in thirds over pressing bar and press to make a

⅜"-wide strip for vines and stems. Cut 4 (42") strips and 4 (36") strips for border vines.

4. Pin vines, leaves, and buds on borders *(Border Diagrams)*. Cut stems of varying lengths from remaining bias.

5. When satisfied with placement, appliqué pieces in place. Add date over rose on bottom border.

6. Sew borders to quilt, mitering corners.

7. Starting at center of each side, measure and mark (with pins) 2⅛"–2¼" sections along raw edge of each red border. (Vary measurements slightly as needed to come out even at corners.) At each mark, make a

Side Border

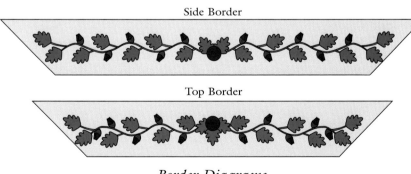

Top Border

Border Diagrams

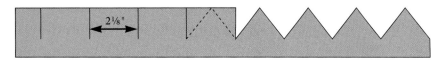

Dogtooth Border Diagram

cut about 1¼" deep—each cut is a valley between teeth *(Dogtooth Border Diagram)*. Fold flaps of each point under to make a triangle; appliqué on cream border. At corners, appliqué scraps of red fabric in place to cover raw edge at mitered seam. Complete appliqué for 8 dogtooth borders.

Quilting and Finishing
Outline-quilt around appliqués. Fill center of each block with a ⅜" grid and background with a ¾" diagonal grid. Quilt leaf detail with green thread. Fill border background with vertical lines ¾" apart.

Bind with straight-grain or bias binding made from red 1.

❖QUILT SMART❖

Ruched Roses

1. Fold over ¼" on long edges of each red strip, wrong sides facing. Raw edges should meet at center *(Diagram 1)*. Baste.
2. Lay strip faceup on *Marking Guide*. Mark dots along folded edges 1" apart as indicated along full length of strip.
3. Hand-sew a gathering stitch from dot to dot, taking

a stitch over folded edge each time you change direction *(Diagram 2)*.
4. Stop to gather strip about every 8". Pull thread, gathering petals on both sides of strip *(Diagram 3)*. Continue for full length of red strip.
5. Using another needle and thread, turn under 1 end of strip and secure. Work first 5 or 6 petals in a tight circle and tack *(Diagram 4)*. Arrange next row

slightly under first circle. Turn flower to wrong side and tack petals to previous row *(Diagram 5)*. Work gathers around, tacking each row in place.
6. On last petal, pull gathering thread tight and knot. Tuck end under flower. Gathered rose should be approximately same circumference as B circle.

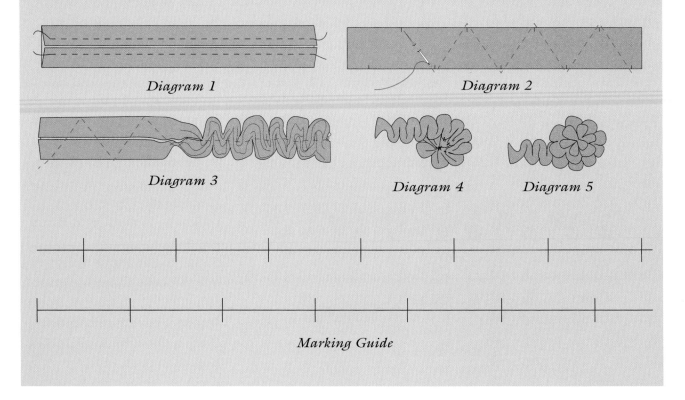

Diagram 1

Diagram 2

Diagram 3

Diagram 4

Diagram 5

Marking Guide

118

A

B

C

7

45

68

1

29

30

119

Designer Gallery

Lura Schwarz Smith
Coarsegold, California

*A*s a teenager, Lura Schwarz Smith made "very bad" quilts with her mother. But they got better as she matured. In college, her senior art project was a quilt.

"Quilting is by far the most satisfying work."

"Quilting evolved from a pleasant pastime to become the central focus of my artistic interests," Lura says. "I also do graphic and illustration work, but quilting is by far the most satisfying and personal work."

Lura combines traditional quiltmaking techniques with her art training. The challenge is to find new ways to get imagery onto fabric. "My favorite techniques recently are free-form machine quilting and photocopying onto fabric," Lura says. She also paints on fabric to create details such as facial features and hair.

Lura's awards, publications, and exhibits are numerous. She is a member of Studio Art Quilt Associates and Sierra Mountain Quilt Association of Oakhurst.

All Up in the Air
1993

To make a guild's challenge quilt, Lura Smith received a set of preselected fabrics. The prints suggested a carnival to Lura, so she used them to create a merry juggler.

"I was under the gun, making this in a hurry," Lura remembers. "I was thinking about how we do the superwoman act—juggling work, personal lives, and children." The idea was so clear in Lura's mind, the quilt seemed to fall into place.

The quilt now belongs to Lura's daughter, who was the model for the juggler.

Seams a Lot Like Degas
1996

"I love the work of the French impressionist Edgar Degas," Lura Smith says, "so this is my homage to his dancers series."

Lura started this piece with an original drawing. Parts of the drawing were photocopied onto fabric, which were then painted and appliquéd onto a machine-pieced background. The appliqué and quilting are done by hand.

Lura made the quilt especially for the Artistic Expressions competition sponsored by *Quilter's Newsletter Magazine* in 1996. Quilters were challenged to create an original quilt inspired by a master artist. *Seams a Lot Like Degas* was judged Best of Show.

Pauline Salzman
Treasure Island, Florida

Before 1991, Pauline Salzman didn't sew anything that she couldn't wear. The owner of a sewing machine dealership, she discovered quilting and it changed her life.

Pauline sold her business in 1991 "because I wanted more time to quilt," she says. But soon she realized "there were only so many bed quilts I could make." So Pauline turned to making story quilts.

"For me, quilts have to tell a story."

"For me, quilts have to tell a story," Pauline says. "Happy, sad, or informative—my quilts need to *say* something."

Pauline believes in always learning and teaching about quilting. Taking classes is important "because I always learn something new . . . it's a way of expanding my horizons."

Teaching quilting can be even more rewarding. Harriet is a friend Pauline met at a nursing home where she brings her dog, Coco, to visit patients. Harriet kept busy doing needlepoint, but Pauline convinced her to try quilting. Harriet is now on her third quilt and loving it—proof that you're never too old to be a quiltmaker.

Pauline's story quilts have won many awards at national shows and one, *In Memory Of . . .*, is in the permanent collection of the Holocaust Museum at St. Petersburg, Florida. She is a member of the Suncoast Quilting Circle and the Largo Crackers.

Snowbirds
1996

Every year, a peculiar bird leaves the cold, windy towns of the northern states and heads south to the warm, friendly climes of Florida. The land of sunny beaches and citrus greets the annual flock of "snowbirds" just after Halloween and sends them home again in time for Easter.

This is the tale told by Pauline Salzman's story quilt, *Snowbirds*. A Detroit native, Pauline made the trip herself in 1967 and stayed.

The quilt depicts Pauline's mother, driving over hill and dale in her pink "land yacht." Pauline used a novelty print to represent other people as flying geese going south.

From its snow-capped mountains to the beachfront condominiums, *Snowbirds* is a humorous take on a Florida phenomenon. The quilt has amused viewers at the Miami Quilt Fest and the Houston International Quilt Festival.

Gerry Sweem
Reseda, California

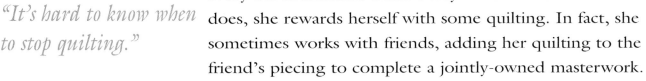

Gerry Sweem quilts every day, even if it's only in her mind.

"If I'm not actually quilting, I'm thinking about what I'll be doing next," Gerry says.

Handwork is Gerry's real love. Appliqué and quilting are her favorites. "I don't much like sitting at the machine—I find that rather tiring," Gerry says. For

"It's hard to know when to stop quilting."

every bit of machine work Gerry does, she rewards herself with some quilting. In fact, she sometimes works with friends, adding her quilting to the friend's piecing to complete a jointly-owned masterwork.

Gerry began quilting in 1975 when she took a class from Sandi Fox. Now that her children are grown and she's on her own when her husband travels, Gerry spends many a pleasant day quilting and quilting and quilting. On quilts like *Little Sister Revisited,* "it's hard to know when to stop quilting," she says.

Gerry is a member of the San Fernando Valley Quilt Guild. She is also one of the SOB Sisters, a small group that has been meeting twice a month for more than 10 years. The Sisters are currently working on a second batch of round-robin quilts.

Little Sister Revisited
1998

Christmas cards bring words of good cheer and New Year's greetings to most people. For Gerry Sweem, one card brought a flash of inspiration.

A few years ago, Gerry received a very special card. On its face was a glorious red and green quilt, illuminated with a cheddar-colored sunburst in its center.

Little Sister's Quilt is part of the Smithsonian Museum's collection of 19th-century quilts. Made before the Civil War, the quilt belonged to Susan Theresa Holbert of Chester, New York, who may also have made the quilt. Its photo on a Christmas card inspired Gerry to create a new, updated version.

A friend, Susan Rossi, drafted a pattern for the quilt on her computer. After the initial piecing of the sunburst was complete, Gerry set out to add her own touches, changing the corner motifs from Carolina Lily blocks in the original to folk-art-style fantasy flowers. She also changed the stars around the center motif and the outside arched flower vine.

The end result is a quilt that finds its roots in the 19th century but is also uniquely today. And like all of Gerry's work, it is lavishly quilted.

Terri Shinn
Snohomish, Washington

*F*or years, quilting was Terri Shinn's secret identity. The *real* Terri could be seen only in her quilts.

Whatever she was feeling—good or bad—Terri expressed in her quilts. "Working it all out in color, texture, and found objects is so therapeutic, and very rewarding," Terri says.

But after a while, Terri realized that she couldn't look at the depressing pieces or put them out in her home. So now she stays in a good mood by focusing on what she calls "nonsense" quilts—fun, cheerful, and wildly expressive fiber art. These pieces make Terri feel like a child with a new box of crayons—"and you don't have to stay inside the lines!" Terri says, "You can just play and have fun."

"You can just play and have fun."

Terri's taste for unorthodox quilts began in college when she just *had* to have a velvet and satin quilt. "I made a horrible attempt to teach myself," Terri remembers. Since then her skills have improved considerably, but her tastes remain eclectic. Bright sunflowers are a favorite theme and her intricate, expertly pieced quilts have appeared in several national shows and publications, including Oxmoor House books.

Terri is a member of Quilters Anonymous and the Monday Night Bowlers (yes, that's a quilting group), as well as the Association of Pacific Northwest Quilters.

Flapdoodles
1995

Someone once told Terri Shinn, "you have nonsense in your heart." Ever since, she has collected nonsense words and made quilts to fit them.

"Flapdoodles" is a real word that means nonsense. (Another favorite nonsense word is 'gallimaufry,' which is the title of another quilt). And nonsense is the theme of this work, as well as several other pieces Terri has made.

This quilt started with some blocks Terri and some friends had made. "They needed help," Terri remembers, "so I exploded them with jewels, sequins, and three-dimensional stars."

Flapdoodles was juried into the 1996 show of the Association of Pacific Northwest Quilters.

Denise Tallon Havlan
Palos Hills, Illinois

*A*rt and Earth are a potent combination in the hands of a lifelong artist.

"I have a passion for our planet and the living things that inhabit it," says Denise Havlan. She grew up drawing and painting, but now she expresses her passion in fabric.

In 1989, Denise became interested in the graphic use of color in antique Amish quilts. Her own experiments with fabric gave her a new outlet for expressing interest and concern about our world.

Denise researches her subjects at the local library, striving for accuracy and realism in her quilts which "portray living things interacting with their environment." She can be so absorbed in the subject that she doesn't work on anything else until the quilt comes to life.

"I have a passion for our planet."

Denise is a member of Himsdale (Illinois) Salt Creek Quilters and the Professional Art Quilter Alliance.

Matriarch
1998

Women play important and powerful roles in every culture, especially in some African societies.

When Denise Havlan purchased four pieces of fabric from Africa, she was inspired to make a quilt about African women.

Matriarch is a tableau of three women in native dress. The oldest woman stares right at the viewer with strength and confidence. Behind her, the elder daughter looks away, concerned with peripheral matters. But the younger daughter, seated at her mother's feet, also looks directly ahead, indicating that she has the strength to be the next matriarch.

Denise gave mother and younger daughter blue eyes to suggest outside influences that affect once isolated societies in a world seemingly grown smaller.

Denise's sense of realism extends to the smallest details of the figures. Not content to create the shapes of hands and feet, she gave each finger and toe a well-sculpted nail.

Matriarch was judged Best Amateur Entry in the Innovative category at the 1998 Pennsylvania National Quilt Extravaganza.

131

Christine L. Adams
Rockville, Maryland

The dictionary defines collage as an artistic composition made of various materials, an assembly of diverse fragments or ideas. Christine Adams combines found objects with fabric to create quilt collage. Bead-and-button jewelry pays the rent, but it's fiber art that warms her soul.

"For a long time, it was my dream to surround myself with wonderful textures, threads, found

"My cup runneth over with . . . an abundance of enticing ideas."

objects, and whatever else catches my interest," Christine says. "Now my cup runneth over with things that provide an abundance of enticing ideas."

Christine learns new techniques from the artists with whom she shares studio space at Rockville Arts Place. Photo transfer is the latest addition to the battery of objects and techniques with which she embellishes her quilts.

"It's exciting to incorporate techniques borrowed from other media," Christine says. "It enables me to continue this great love affair with fiber that began when I was very young."

Christine is a member of national fiber art and quilters' groups, as well as the Washington area's Fiber Art Study Group.

Our Town
1998

If you live in the Washington, D.C., area, it's easy to get the idea that most Americans think your town is a terrible place. Newscasters say things like, "Washington is raising taxes." In fact, *Washington* doesn't do those things—politicians do. And *all* of them come from someplace *else*.

"I wanted to show that Washington is about more than politics," Christine Adams says. "Washington is a beautiful city, and I wanted to show it in the best way I could—by making a quilt."

Our Town depicts Washington landmarks in a fabric collage. Based on a Parcheesi

board, the quilt acknowledges the buzz that emanates from Capitol Hill in its subtitle: Games People Play.

"Though Washington is always in the national news, people who live here go to work or to school, raise kids, live lives just like in any other town," Christine says. "In that

sense, it's our town, every town. But it's also the nation's capital, and visitors see the monuments, the Smithsonian, and all the wonderful things Washington has to offer."

Christine layered photo transfers on fabric and then used free-motion quilting to secure and embellish the collage. She used images that commemorate important events or principles as well as great men and women who have served the nation.

"Washington will preserve the nation's history when this batch of politicians is gone," Christine says. "But for those who live here, it's our town."

133

Emily Parson
St. Charles, Illinois

*E*mily Parson likes whimsy. She is a serious artist, but that doesn't mean she can't have fun.

Emily uses bold color and a sense of humor to create pictorial quilts that turn everyday objects into larger-than-life tapestries. "I hope my quilts cause people to feel, think, and occasionally, to laugh," she says.

Emily starts with a life-size (or larger) drawing of the subject—a dog, a telephone, or a teapot. Then she creates a collage, layering hundreds of pieces of fabric onto a background. If she can't find the fabric she wants, Emily likes to dye her own vibrant-colored fabrics. The final design element is machine-quilting through all the layers, using quilting motifs that enhance the mood of the appliqué.

"I hope my quilts cause people to feel, to think, and to laugh."

A native of Muncie, Indiana, Emily worked as a clothing designer in New York for several years before turning to quiltmaking full-time. Her quilts have won awards at many national exhibitions and hang in private and corporate collections across the country.

Tea Party
1997

For many people, teapots are precious and sentimental things. You might collect them because they're pretty or because you like the shape. For some people—the British and Japanese, for example—tea time is a cultural ritual.

Emily Parson doesn't drink much tea now, but tea parties were a part of her childhood. "I drank tea and made Easy-Bake Oven pies," she remembers.

In this small quilt, Emily wanted to recapture the feeling of a little girl's fantasy. She imagines this to be like the teapot Alice may have had at the Mad Hatter's tea party in Wonderland.

Tea Party is part of a travelling exhibit, Artistic Teapots, curated by Beth Gilbert.

Lauren Camp
Santa Fe, New Mexico

*M*ost of us quickly give up on New Year's resolutions. In 1993, Lauren Camp resolved to make a quilt, and she fulfilled her resolution before the year was out.

"I quickly learned that I didn't enjoy fussing with the sewing machine," Lauren says. But learning the basic techniques of appliqué "opened a world of opportunity for me, letting me realize visions with a method that is adaptable to unusual shapes." A class in Baltimore Album-style appliqué gave Lauren the skills she needed.

"Now I put them to use in my own designs," she says. "Creating your own designs is both a hardship and a joy, but I treasure each opportunity to create another image—I want to make worlds out of pictures."

"Creating your own designs is both a hardship and a joy."

Lauren had worked with other art forms, but soon began to feel strongly about fabric and quilting. She finds hand appliqué to be "meditative and relaxing." As a designer, "I enjoy working out the decisions in each part of the process," she says. "I also appreciate the struggle of making fine art, having no one but yourself to be accountable to."

Lauren quilts four to six hours a day. After years of working at the kitchen table, she recently rented studio space and is becoming serious about exhibiting her quilts. Her work earned awards at the Fiber Arts Fiesta in Albuquerque and at the 1999 Road to California quilt show.

Twilight Vigil
1997

Lauren Camp was captivated by a fuzzy black and white photograph she found in a book. She adapted the strong rectangular image to create *Twilight Vigil*.

Lauren chose to depict the zebras at sunset, when the dying light plays the animals' black and white stripes into blazing colors. To create a burning African sunset, she had Batiks Etcetera dye the

background fabric to her specifications. Lauren drew on her fabric collection to create the zebras.

The design process started with a photocopy that reduced the photo to a series of bumps and squiggles, making the image seem three-dimensional. "This makes the appliqué more labor-intensive," Lauren says, "but I'm so pleased with the results I get that it's worth it—I want my work to read from across the room, and beg closer inspection."

Lauren used leaf print fabrics on the quilt back as patterns to create the foliage that surrounds the zebras. Working from the back instead of the front, she used a collection of green threads to quilt grasses and leaves.

Making *Twilight Vigil* led Lauren to learn about zebras and their environment. She learned that zebras, like many animals on the African plain, are ever wary of predators. By standing shoulder to shoulder, each staring in a different direction, the herd maintains a complete view of the surroundings and other animals that may approach.

Ann Winterton Seely
Salt Lake City, Utah

*F*ew people enjoy *every* aspect of quilting as much as Ann Seely does. She even likes to wash and press a new piece of fabric. Choosing fabric and piecing are a pleasure, but hand quilting is Ann's bliss.

"We spend weekends at our mountain cabin where I usually have a quilt on the frame," Ann says.

Her sister, Joyce Stewart, introduced Ann to quilting in 1983, when she learned to strip-piece a star quilt.

"I love hand quilting most."

"I have worked on quiltmaking skills, in one way or another, every day since then," she says.

"I enjoy choosing fabric and machine piecing the top," Ann says, "but I love the hand quilting most." This follows Ann's lifelong passion for handwork, adding to her skills of knitting, tatting, and cross-stitch.

With her sister, Ann is the author of a book on use of color in quilts. She is a member of the Utah Quilt Guild.

Cabin Christmas
1997

"I love traditional patterns," Ann Seely says, and that affection is evident in *Cabin Christmas,* a sampler of favorite blocks and motifs.

Ann relishes the quest of finding new settings for traditional blocks. She designed this quilt on a computer, a challenge but "lots of fun."

A classic medallion setting enabled Ann to add row after row of different motifs. Red and green give the quilt a holiday look that cheers the Seely cabin near Park City, Utah.

QUILT SMART WORKSHOP
A Guide to Quiltmaking

Preparing Fabric

Before cutting any pieces, be sure to wash and dry your fabric to preshrink it. All-cotton fabrics may need pressing before cutting. Trim selvages from the fabric before you cut pieces.

Making Templates

Before you can make one of the quilts in this book, you must make templates from the printed patterns given. (Not all pieces require patterns—some pieces are meant to be cut with a rotary cutter and ruler.) Quilters have used many materials to make templates, including cardboard and sandpaper. Transparent template plastic, available at craft supply and quilt shops, is durable, see-through, and easy to use.

To make a plastic template, place the plastic sheet on the printed page and use a laundry marker or permanent fine-tip marking pen to trace each pattern. For machine piecing, trace on the outside solid (cutting) line. For hand piecing, trace on the inside broken (stitching) line. Cut out the template on the traced line. Label each template with the pattern name, letter, grain line arrow, and match points (corner dots).

Marking and Cutting Fabric for Piecing

Place the template facedown on the wrong side of the fabric and mark around it with a sharp pencil.

If you will be piecing by machine, the pencil lines represent cutting lines. Cut on each marked line.

For hand piecing, the pencil lines are seam lines. Leave at least ¾" between marked lines for seam allowances. Add ¼" seam allowance around each piece as you cut. Mark match points (corner dots) on each piece.

You can do without templates if you use a rotary cutter and ruler to cut straight strips and geometric shapes such as squares and triangles. Rotary cutting is always paired with machine piecing, and pieces are cut with seam allowances included.

Hand Piecing

To hand piece, place two fabric pieces together with right sides facing. Insert a pin in each match point of the top piece. Stick the pin through both pieces and check to be sure that it pierces the match point on the bottom piece (*Figure 1*). Adjust the pieces as necessary to align the match points. (The raw edges of the two pieces may not align exactly.) Pin the pieces securely together.

Sew with a running stitch of 8 to 10 stitches per inch. Sew from match point to match point, checking the stitching as you go to be sure you are sewing in the seam line of both pieces.

To make sharp corners, begin and end the stitching exactly at the match point; do not stitch into the seam allowances. When joining units where several seams come together, do not sew over seam allowances; sew through them at the point where all seam lines meet (*Figure 2*).

Always press both seam allowances to one side. Pressing the seam open, as in dressmaking, can leave gaps between stitches through which the batting may beard. Press seam allowances toward the darker fabric whenever you can, but it is sometimes more important to reduce bulk by avoiding overlapping seam allowances. When four or more seams meet at one point, such as at the corner of a block, press all the seams in a "swirl" in the same direction to reduce bulk (*Figure 3*).

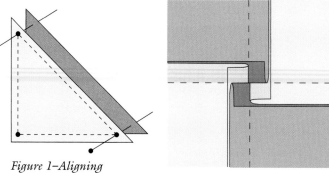

Figure 1–Aligning Match Points

Figure 3–Pressing Intersecting Seams

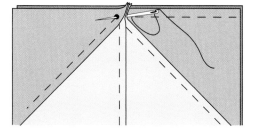

Figure 2–Joining Units

Machine Piecing

To machine piece, place two fabric pieces together with right sides facing. Align match points as described under "Hand Piecing" and pin the pieces together securely.

Set the stitch length at 12 to 15 stitches per inch. At this setting, you do not need to backstitch to lock seam beginnings and ends. Use a presser foot that gives a perfect ¼" seam allowance, or measure ¼" from the needle and mark that point on the presser foot with nail polish or masking tape.

Chain piecing, stitching edge to edge, saves time when sewing similar sets of pieces (*Figure 4*). Join the first two pieces as usual. At the end of the seam, do not backstitch, cut the thread, or lift the presser foot. Instead, sew a few stitches off the fabric. Place the next two pieces and continue stitching. Keep sewing until all the sets are joined. Then cut the sets apart.

Press seam allowances toward the darker fabric whenever possible. When you join blocks or rows, press the seam allowances of the top row in one direction and the seam allowances of the bottom row in the opposite direction to help ensure that the seams will lie flat (*Figure 5*).

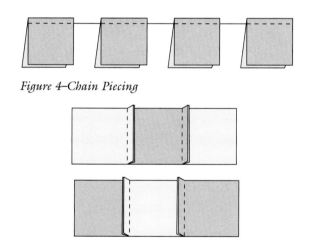

Figure 4–Chain Piecing

Figure 5–Pressing Seams for Machine Piecing

Hand Appliqué

Hand appliqué is the best way to achieve the look of traditional appliqué. However, using freezer paper, which is sold in grocery stores, saves a lot of time because it eliminates the need for hand basting the seam allowances.

Make templates without seam allowances. Trace the template onto the *dull* side of the freezer paper and cut the paper on the marked line. Make a freez-er-paper shape for each piece to be appliquéd.

Pin the freezer-paper shape, *shiny side up*, to the *wrong side* of the fabric. Following the paper shape and adding a scant ¼" seam allowance, cut out the fabric piece. Do not remove the pins. Use the tip of a hot, dry iron to press the seam allowance to the shiny side of the freezer paper. Be careful not to touch the shiny side of the freezer paper with the iron. Remove the pins.

Pin the appliqué shape in place on the background fabric. Use one strand of sewing thread in a color to match the appliqué shape. Using a very small slipstitch (*Figure 6*) or blindstitch (*Figure 7*), appliqué the shape to the background fabric.

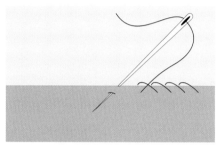

Figure 6–Slipstitch

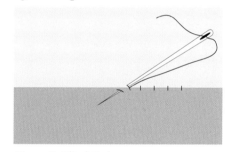

Figure 7–Blindstitch

When your stitching is complete, cut away the background fabric behind the appliqué, leaving ¼" seam allowance. Separate the freezer paper from the fabric with your fingernail and pull gently to remove it.

Mitering Borders

Mitered borders take a little extra care to stitch but offer a nice finish when square border corners just won't do.

First, measure the length of the quilt through the middle of the quilt top. Cut two border strips to fit this length, plus the width of the border plus 2". Centering the measurement on the strip, place pins on the edge of each strip at the center and each end of the measurement. Match the pins on each border strip to the corners of a long side of the quilt.

Starting and stopping ¼" from each corner of the quilt, sew the borders to the quilt, easing the quilt to fit between the pins (*Figure 8*). Press seam allowances toward border strip.

Measure the quilt width through the middle and cut two border strips to fit, adding the border width plus 2". Join these borders to opposite ends of the quilt in the same manner.

Fold one border corner over the adjacent corner (*Figure 9*) and press. On the wrong side, stitch in the creased fold to stitch a mitered seam (*Figure 10*). Press; then check to make sure the corner lies flat on the quilt top. Trim seam allowances.

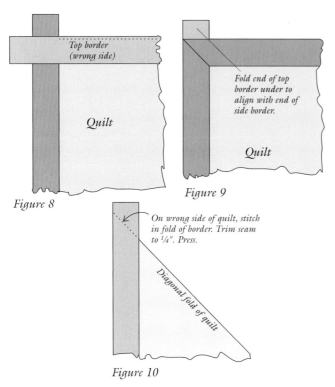

Figure 8

Figure 9

Figure 10

Mitering Borders

Marking Your Quilt Top

When the quilt top is complete, press it thoroughly before marking it with quilting designs. The most popular methods for marking use stencils or templates. Both can be purchased, or you can make your own (see Quilt Smart, page 99). You can also use a yardstick to mark straight lines or grids.

Use a silver quilter's pencil for marking light to medium fabrics and a white chalk pencil on dark fabrics. Lightly mark the quilt top with your chosen quilting designs.

Making a Backing

The instructions in *Great American Quilts* give backing yardage based on 45"-wide fabric unless a 90"-wide or 108"-wide backing is more practical. (These fabrics are sold at fabric and quilt shops.) Pieced or not, the quilt backing should be at least 3" larger on all sides than the quilt top.

Backing fabric should be of a type and color that is compatible with the quilt top. Percale sheets are not recommended, because they are tightly woven and difficult to hand-quilt through.

A pieced backing for a bed quilt should have three panels. The three-panel backing is recommended because it tends to wear better and lie flatter than the two-panel type, the center seam of which often makes a ridge down the center of the quilt. Begin by cutting the fabric in half widthwise (*Figure 11*). Open the two lengths and stack them, with right sides facing and selvages aligned. Stitch along both selvage edges to create a tube of fabric (*Figure 12*). Cut down the center of the top layer of fabric *only* and open the fabric flat (*Figure 13*). Press seam allowances toward center panel.

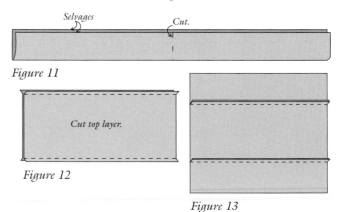

Figure 11

Figure 12

Figure 13

Making a Three-Panel Backing

Layering and Basting

Prepare a working surface to spread out the quilt. Place the backing on the surface, right side down. Unfold the batting and place it on top of the backing. Smooth any wrinkles or lumps in the batting. Lay the quilt top right side up on top of the batting and backing. Make sure backing and quilt top are parallel.

Use a darning needle for basting, with a long strand of sewing thread. Begin in the center of your quilt and baste out toward the edges. The stitches should cover enough of the quilt to keep the layers from shifting during quilting. Inadequate basting can result in puckers and folds on the back and front of the quilt during quilting.

Hand Quilting

Hand quilting can be done with the quilt in a hoop or in a floor frame. It is best to start in the middle of your quilt and quilt out toward the edges.

Most quilters use a thin, short needle called a "between." Betweens are available in sizes 7 to 12, with 7 being the longest and 12 the shortest. If you are a beginning quilter, try a size 7 or 8. Because betweens are so much shorter than other needles, they may feel awkward at first. As your skill increases, try using a smaller needle to help you make smaller stitches.

Quilting thread, heavier and stronger than sewing thread, is available in a wide variety of colors. If color matching is critical and you can't find the color you need, you can substitute cotton sewing thread if you coat it with beeswax before quilting to prevent it from tangling.

Thread your needle with a 20" length and make a small knot at one end. Insert the needle into the quilt top approximately ½" from the point where you want to begin quilting. Do not take the needle through all three layers, but stop it in the batting and bring it up through the quilt top again at your starting point. Tug gently on the thread to pop the knot through the quilt top into the batting. This anchors the thread without an unsightly knot showing on the back.

With your non-sewing hand underneath the quilt, insert the needle with the point straight down in the quilt about ¹⁄₁₆" from the starting point. With your underneath finger, feel for the point as the needle comes through the backing (*Figure 14*). Place the thumb of your sewing hand approximately ½" ahead of the needle. When you feel the needle touch your underneath finger, push the fabric up from below as you rock the needle down to a nearly horizontal position. Using the thumb of your sewing hand in conjunction with the underneath hand, pinch a little hill in the fabric and push the tip of the needle back through the quilt top (*Figure 15*).

Now either push the needle all the way through to complete one stitch or rock the needle again to

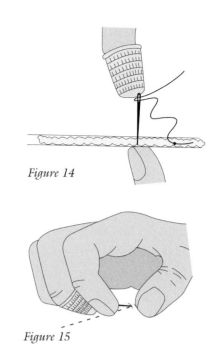

Figure 14

Figure 15

Hand Quilting

an upright position on its point to take another stitch. Take no more than a quarter-needleful of stitches before pulling the needle through.

When you have 6" of thread remaining, you must end the old thread securely and invisibly. Carefully tie a knot in the thread, flat against the surface of the fabric. Pop the knot through the top as you did when beginning the line of quilting. Clip the thread, rethread your needle, and continue quilting.

Machine Quilting

Machine quilting is as old as the sewing machine itself; but until recently, it was thought inferior to hand quilting. Exquisite stitching like the quilting on *Tie a Yellow Ribbon* (page 100) puts fine machine quilting in an exclusive category, but it requires a different set of skills from hand quilting.

Machine quilting can be done on your sewing machine using a straight stitch and a special presser foot. A walking foot or even-feed foot is recommended for straight-line quilting to help the top fabric move through the machine at the same rate that the feed dogs move the bottom fabric.

Regular sewing thread or nylon thread can be used for machine quilting. With the quilt top facing you, roll the long edges of the basted quilt toward the center, leaving a 12"-wide area unrolled in the center. Secure the roll with bicycle clips, metal bands that are available at quilt shops. Begin at one unrolled end and fold the quilt over and over until only a small area is showing. This will be the area where you will begin to quilt.

Place the folded portion of the quilt in your lap. Start quilting in the center and work to the right, unfolding and unrolling the quilt as you go. Remove the quilt from the machine, turn it, and reinsert it in the machine to stitch the left side. A table placed behind your sewing machine will help support the quilt as it is stitched.

Curves and circles are most easily made by free-motion machine quilting. Using a darning foot and with the feed dogs down, move the quilt under the needle with your fingertips. Place your hands on the fabric on each side of the foot and run the machine at a steady, medium speed. The length of the stitches is determined by the rate of speed at which you move fabric through the machine. Do not rotate the quilt; rather, move it from side to side as needed. Always stop with the needle down to keep the quilt from shifting.

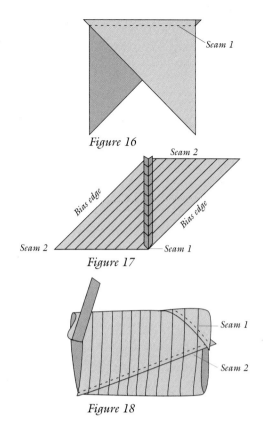

Figure 16

Figure 17

Figure 18

Continuous Bias Binding

Making Binding

A continuous bias or straight-grain strip is used to bind quilt edges. Bias binding is especially recommended for quilts with curved edges. Follow these steps to make a continuous bias strip:

1. Start with a square of fabric. Multiply the number of binding inches needed by the cut width of the binding strip (usually 2½"). Use a calculator to find the square root of that number. That's the size of the fabric square needed to make your binding.
2. Cut the square in half diagonally.
3. With right sides facing, join triangles to form a sawtooth as shown (Figure 16).
4. Press seam open. Mark off parallel lines the desired width of the binding as shown (Figure 17).
5. With right sides facing, align raw edges marked Seam 2. Offset edges by one strip width, so one side is higher than the other (Figure 18). Stitch Seam 2. Press seam open.
6. Cut the binding in a continuous strip, starting with the protruding point and following the marked lines around the tube.
7. Press the binding strip in half lengthwise, with wrong sides facing.

Attaching Binding

To prepare your quilt for binding, baste the layers together ¼" from the edge of the quilt. Trim the backing and batting even with the edge of the quilt top. Beginning at the midpoint of one side of the quilt, pin the binding to the top, with right sides facing and raw edges aligned.

Machine-stitch the binding along one edge of the quilt, sewing through all layers. Backstitch at the beginning of the seam to lock the stitching.

Stitch until you reach the seam line at the corner, and backstitch. Lift the presser foot and turn the quilt to align the foot with the next edge. Continue sewing around all four sides. Join the beginning and end of the binding strip by machine, or stitch one end by hand to overlap the other.

Turn the binding over the edge and blindstitch it in place on the backing. At each corner, fold the excess binding neatly to make a mitered corner and blindstitch it in place.